Praise for Joseph Ca..... ....

"My thanks to Joe Cardillo for keeping the flame of martial arts burning brightly."

—Joe Hyams, author of *Zen in the Martial Arts*

"Cardillo teaches us, with his graceful approach, how to focus, concentrate, and connect with our core energy to generate harmony, self-confidence, and love. *Bow to Life* is a perfect companion to help guide us through life's daily challenges."

—Nancy O'Hara, author of *Find a Quiet Corner* and *Just Listen*

"Joseph Cardillo guides the reader on an exciting passageway of new discoveries, ultimately leading to a more refined method for encountering and interacting with life."

—Scott Shaw, author of *Nirvana in a Nutshell*

HOW TO THINK FAST,
FIND YOUR FOCUS, AND SHARPEN
YOUR CONCENTRATION

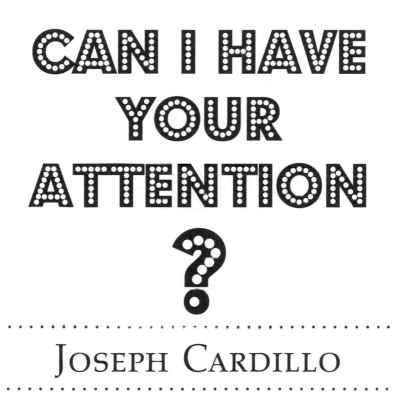

CAN I HAVE YOUR ATTENTION?

JOSEPH CARDILLO

CAREER
PRESS

Franklin Lakes, N.J.

CAN I HAVE YOUR ATTENTION?
EDITED AND TYPESET BY KARA KUMPEL
Cover design by Howard Grossman/12E Design
Printed in the U.S.A. by Book-mart Press

To order this title, please call toll-free 1-800-CAREER-1 (NJ and Canada: 201-848-0310) to order using VISA or MasterCard, or for further information on books from Career Press.

The Career Press, Inc., 3 Tice Road, PO Box 687,
Franklin Lakes, NJ 07417
www.careerpress.com

Library of Congress Cataloging-in-Publication Data
Cardillo, Joe, 1951–
    Can I have your attention? : how to think fast, find your focus, and sharpen your concentration / by Joseph Cardillo.
        p. cm.
    Includes index.
    ISBN 978-1-60163-063-6
    1. Attention. I. Title.

BF321.C37 2009
153.7'33—dc22

                                                            2009007688

DEDICATION

For our daughter, Veronica.
We have loved you since before you were born.

ACKNOWLEDGMENTS

I wish to thank my immediate family and extended family for their energies and guidance in helping bring this project to completion.

Special thanks are extended to my wife, Elaine, for her love, friendship, and support through this journey; and to our daughters, Isabella and Veronica, for all their goodness and magnificence.

I want to also convey my gratitude to the scientists and scholars who agreed to tell me about their amazing work and answer my many questions about the workings of human attention. Special thanks to: Dr. Lydia Furman, Dr. James Diefendorff, Dr. Stanley Glick, Dr. Robert Josephs, Dr. Deirdre V. Lovecky, Dr. John Mayer, Sergeant Michael McLaren, Colonel Kevin Nally, Dr. Tram Neill, Dr. Donald Pfaff, Dr. Todd Rasner, Dr. Frank Vellutino, Dr. Donald Ward, Dr. Christian Wheeler, Dr. Wythe Whiting, and Dr. Todd Wysocki.

Thanks to Matthew Papa as well as all my martial arts associates, partners, and colleagues for their support, brotherhood, and sisterhood.

I am also deeply indebted to the hard work and brilliant research of the many scientists and scholars whose research was noted in these pages. Without their tremendous and admirable work a book like this would not be possible.

Special thanks are also extended to my agent, Linda Konner; to my publicist, Robin Waxenburg; and everyone at Career Press/ New Page Books, especially Ron Fry, Michael Pye, Laurie Kelly-Pye, Kristen Parkes, Kirsten Dalley, Kara Kumpel, Jeff Piasky, Diana Ghazzawi, and Allison Olson, for their terrific commitment to the vision of this project. Thanks also to the publicity team at Newman Communications.

It is with deep gratitude that I acknowledge my parents, Alfio and Josephine Cardillo, for their gifts of love and encouragement, and life.

As humans we are formed to pay attention.
Without it, we simply would not survive.
—Maggie Jackson, author of *Distracted*

CONTENTS

INTRODUCTION

Knowing something about the mechanics of your attention can be as powerful as any therapy or medication or drug.
—Steven Johnson, author of *Mind Wide Open*

Attention plays a critical role in nearly every choice you make. Connected to the very essence of your being, your brain's attention mechanism is hardwired to help you become everything that you can be. As such, you cannot be who you really want to be unless this mechanism functions properly. This is because your attentional system can determine what you think, what emotions you feel, and what behaviors you engage in. It can affect your motivation as well as the achievement of imminent and longer-range goals. The way you attend to things will either help you or hurt you with day-to-day goals, whether at work, at home, in your marriage, parenting and other relationships, or in areas of health, academics, recreation, creativity, or even spirituality. It will determine how you experience pain or pleasure and if you feel scattered or focused, distressed or calm, depressed or spirited, and whether you are prone to anger or contentment.

Ideas about attention first trickled down from philosophies rooted in a myriad of world traditions, some of these established many years before the foundation of psychology itself. In martial arts tradition, for example, tenets relating to alertness and focus can be traced back to A.D. 525 when a Buddhist monk named Bodidharma visited the Shaolin Temple of China and taught the monks who lived there meditation, breathing, and a host of other skills to generate greater mental clarity and physical alertness as well as more authentic, enlightened living.

Centuries later, in 1890, psychologist William James—who spearheaded psychological research in this country—maintained that attention is at the very root of human judgment, character, and will. Of the early psychologists, James's definition of attention is perhaps the one most quoted. According to him, attention is "taking possession by the mind, in clear and vivid form, of one out of what seem like several simultaneous objects or trains of thought." James further theorized that attention involved your ability to withdraw focus from certain things so that you could pay attention to something else. Philosophically speaking, James's view was not all that different from the one held by martial and other holistic arts for more than a millennium, but his insistence that attention could be understood, especially in terms of how it functioned, did carve the way for much scientific research that followed. James had more or less understood what science would later discover was at least one component within the inner workings of attention. And even though we know much more about attention today, James's early notions not only helped aim scientists in the right direction, but also encouraged further research to try to demystify this powerful mental capacity. This is important because it jettisoned attention from its usual domain within the realm of artists and mystics and began to address it as a skill—endowed as a birthright to all humans—which, like all skills, could be learned and developed.

Until recently, however, we have not had the tools to drive such ideas as those held by William James beyond speculation. But with the advent of refined neuroimaging equipment and techniques and owing a lot to researchers in the neuroworld, we now know a lot more about the brain's role in how we attend and how our attentional mechanism is linked to practically everything we do in life, from intellectual achievements to work, relationships, and who we each are as a person.

We now have scientific evidence that a person's attentional skill correlates to all levels of successful living.

Following this path of evidence, *Can I Have Your Attention?* is not your traditional self-help book that offers 12 simple steps to enhance brainpower, nor is it a book on Eastern wisdom, spirituality, or conventional meditation. What it is is a book that will take you on an eye-popping adventure that combines ancient, high-speed attention-building processes with frontier attention research in psychology, neurology, and biology.

For example, did you know that:

- You can use your attention to create procedures (capable of triggering in milliseconds) to help perfect any daily activity—from piano playing to work-related activities to perfecting your golf swing?

- In just one-six-hundredth of a second, a random detail you catch from the corner of your eye can determine whether or not you like someone you just met, cause or avoid an accident, feel happy or depressed for the entire day, and succeed or fail at anything you try?

- Specifically designed meditation techniques can be used to scan and shift brainwaves, altering one's attention as effectively as electrode-packed biofeedback instruments?

All-importantly, you can train your attention to turn such processes on or off upon command.

As such, *Can I Have Your Attention?* proceeds from the understanding that knowing just a little bit about how the brain's attention mechanism works can help you free up your mental hard drive and lead to faster, sharper, more targeted thinking and focal power.

By the end of this book, you will have learned many techniques for self-regulating this tantalizing and vital brain mechanism. You will further discover that in the world of brain science, self-regulation is becoming the name of the game for goal management in every aspect of life—professional, interpersonal, academic, recreational, and even medical. The best news is that you don't have to have a PhD or an MD to begin your own attention training program. Just knowing the basics of what goes on in your own head as you try to tend to things throughout the day can make a big difference.

In *Can I Have Your Attention?* you will meet creative individuals, cutting-edge scientists, athletes, top-level military personnel, medical personnel, martial artists, and others, of all ages, who help provide the full picture of attention skills. You will travel from the peaks of China's Sung Mountains to electrode-packed caps and national newsrooms of Presidential Election 2008. You will listen to the whoosh of a blistery, winter morning's lesson in ancient breathing techniques, discover what's really behind the word *attention* in the U.S. Marine Corps, learn how to tap into the high-speed processing of your own mind, and more. *The book's conclusion will present a redefinition of attention deficit, as well as reveal a variety of natural, nonmedical tools that can significantly amp up attention.* Be ready for some real and useful surprises.

1

CAN I HAVE YOUR ATTENTION?

*Clearly if we were to enhance our faculty of attention,
our lives would improve dramatically.*
—B. Alan Wallace, author of *The Attention Revolution:
Unlocking the Power of the Focused Mind*

My Attention Is Mine

Not long ago I was in the kitchen getting together a pot of morning coffee when my 3-year-old daughter, Isabella, pranced into the room wearing a pink ballerina tutu and pirouetted across the floor. It was early, somewhere around 6 a.m.

Delighted by her spunk and happiness, I stopped what I was doing and bid her good morning. I complimented her dance moves and then added that she should look out for a large toy car that her younger sister had left parked on the floor. She seemed a little— *oblivious* is the word that comes to mind—to what I was saying. Instead of acknowledging what I'd said, she told me that she was "dancing with her heart."

I enjoyed hearing this. I complimented her again and once more warned her about the car. It certainly appeared she wasn't paying attention. So I asked, a little concerned, "Isabella, may I please have your attention?"

She responded, "But Daddy, that's not possible."

Well, I thought, she had heard me; apparently she hadn't been oblivious. At that moment, the old TV show *Kids Say the Darnest Things* came to mind. I decided to conduct a little experiment, and, amused, asked, "And why can't you give me your attention?"

"Because," she whispered, as if she was letting me in on a big secret, "my attention is mine, so I *can't* give it to anybody else."

I considered the technical implications of what she had said and thought, well, she might have a point. As a writer and father, I couldn't help being proud of my daughter's verbal skills. I recalled the book *All I Really Need to Know I Learned in Kindergarten*. The romantic part of me wanted to consider my daughter's off-the-cuff comment about attention a gift from the gods, a stroke of childhood genius that had been handed to me on a silver platter; coincidentally, I was in the middle of writing a book about how to improve thinking and attention. Certainly a lot of popular culture would, unbeknownst to Isabella, agree with her statement. The anthem *my mind is my mind and nobody else's* echoes everywhere from rock 'n' roll to kids' cartoons. J.D. Salinger captured the attitude in his classic novel, *The Catcher in the Rye*, which is loaded with questions such as: Don't we all come into life with a clean slate of attention? Isn't your attention exclusively yours, and shouldn't it be? Doesn't your "clean slate" get contaminated with age? And isn't your life-long job resetting your mind to its clean, default settings? Or are we doomed to fly off the proverbial cliff and lose what mental control we still have left, as hero Holden Caulfield describes what happens to us all in growing up?

Certainly the idea of keeping a youthful mind isn't anything new. Nor is the idea of making your mind your own. But could rinsing your mind free of contaminants make you think faster, sharper, and even more authentically as you age? And if so, how would you do it? My daughter's whimsical response had sent me reeling, thinking of the possibilities.

The educator part of me cautioned not to jump the gun on the idea; 28 years of college teaching had steeped me in the scientific method—I was used to asking tough questions and requiring more proof. My training as a martial artist also urged me to push on the breaks. In fact, there is a chief martial arts tenet that says your life's job is to attain a youthful body and a 100-year-old mind. This certainly appeared the opposite of keeping a "youthful mind." Nevertheless, I found something intriguing in my daughter's take on attention, even if it might turn out to be just an interesting accident of words.

I mentioned the episode to a few colleagues at the college where I teach, and they received it with much pleasure—and also the strong suggestion that there may be more to Isabella's offhand comment than meets the eye.

A few days later, I set out to see what I could discover. My search began with contacting a group of top-level psychologists and sharing Isabella's story with them. But I have to say that approaching such men and women to ask if there is any connection among something your 3-year-old has said, cutting-edge research in their field, and a book you are writing on quickening and sharpening the adult mind could tend to make one feel a little anxious. Nonetheless, everyone loved Isabella's lively take on attention, and after a few good chuckles we all hunkered down to take a closer look at the subject. If nothing else, I believed, the discussions would give me a better peek into the brains of my children, as well as into my own.

Stop Thinking and Just Pay Attention

My interest in the mechanics of attention and linking it to high-speed, accurate thinking began 25 years earlier, during the early stages of my martial arts training, although at that point my goals were primarily to improve in my sport. As do most martial arts students, I spent the majority of my time learning and refining complex physical techniques and movements. Only occasionally did a sensei ("instructor," in Japanese) hint that there may be other lessons to be mastered.

One day, however, my instructor noticed me stressing to remember the movements in a kata, a sequence of martial arts postures that looks like a dance, that I was practicing. I wanted to perform the kata powerfully and gracefully, but I found myself having to stop and think about each posture before doing it. Was it right-hand first or left-hand first? Did I take one or two steps forward?

"Stop thinking and just pay attention," my teacher said.

There was that word: *attention*. Little did I know that this word (and skill) that I believed I already understood would become the key to many levels of success in my life, and perhaps one of the most important skills I would ever hone. But first, similar to everybody else, I would have to change my understanding of what *attention* meant and how to use it. Up until then, I had thought of *attention* as synonymous with *concentrating* or *thinking*. But my sensei was out to change that.

I nodded, letting my teacher know that I had heard him. But seconds later, when I thought about what he'd said, I was confused. Had I heard him correctly? *How can you pay attention to anything if you stop thinking?*

That afternoon when I went home I was still thinking about what my instructor had said. So I decided to test his advice. It was a beautiful late-autumn afternoon. The air was cidery and the sky big. The first snow wasn't that far away. I scanned the field behind my house. There were several cords of firewood I'd been stacking for weeks and mounds of fallen leaves beginning to pile up around them. I decided to do some raking. I gave the job my full concentration. I remembered what my teacher had said about attention and tried to absorb as much detail as possible. I still didn't understand how you could pay attention without thinking, but I was willing to give it a whirl. I kept concentrating. Nevertheless, instead of voiding my thoughts, it felt as though a switch had turned on in my head that made me think even more. In fact, I became so wrapped up in my thoughts about leaves, colors, patterns, and such that I completely lost touch with what I was doing—raking leaves. My grand finale was tripping in a pothole that had been excavated by our pet dog. Well, I thought, so much for my little test. What good was paying attention that way?

"Not much," my instructor commented later that week when I told him about the incident.

He noticed how puzzled I was and laughed. "It's like when you're playing tennis and the ball is coming at you faster than a car or someone throws a lightning-fast roundhouse kick at your head. You are alert. You see it coming. You make decisions, you react— fast. It just happens. Ever watch an Olympic skier making adjustments as she flies downhill? Or a tennis pro running around the court making what look like superhuman shots? They just lay into it. It's automatic."

My sensei was describing a state of mind the Japanese call *mushin*, which literally means "no mind." According to the ancient masters, mushin is operating when your mind's attention moves from one activity to another, without the interference of thought. Your mind flows like a stream of hyper-alert water, filling every space in your environment. Mushin is a coveted state of mind all martial artists strive to reach.

My teacher took a deep breath and looked at me. "I'm not telling you to stop thinking completely and forever," he added.

He just wanted me to think a lot less. That way, he explained, when I did think, it would be fast and efficient, unfettered by the usual bundles of other thoughts.

He could see I was still confused. "When you're 'lost' in one of those movies you like watching you are not really lost, are you? Your mind is open wide and you are actually very aware. You are relaxed and paying attention to everything on the screen. You're right there, but not thinking about it. Once in a while you pause to think, and your mind stops. When that happens, you are there with your thought, but then you have lost sight of what's happening on the screen. Do you see?"

"Is that a bad thing?" I asked.

"Yes *and* no," he said. "It's all in what you are giving up."

Miyamoto Musashi

To help me better understand how to use *mushin* to quicken my mind, my instructor told me a story about a famous Japanese swordsman named Miyamoto Musashi. According to Miyamoto, your attention must always be in a state of flowing. If it stops anywhere, the flow is interrupted, and it is this interruption that deteriorates your attention. In the case of the swordsman, deterioration of attention meant death. Musashi teaches that when a swordsman stands against an opponent, he is not to think about his enemy, himself, or the movement of swords. He must think of nothing and let what is in the unconscious surface and take over.

Hollywood shares Musashi's lesson of mushin in the movie *The Last Samurai*. The film focuses on a group of samurai warriors led by the swordsman Katsumoto. Nathan Algren, played by Tom Cruise, is an American who has been captured in battle by the samurai. As time passes Cruise becomes enamored by his captors' physical and mental strength as well as their incredible swordsmanship. Before long, he is trying to shed the less wholesome ways of his past and become more like the samurai. In the scene that involves mushin, Algren is learning how to wield a sword. He has just been defeated in sparring yet again by Nobutada, Katsumoto's son. Algren is on the ground and is approached by Nobutada, who tries to explain why Algren keeps losing. "Please forgive," he says. "You have too many mind."

Algren questions what Nobutada means: "Too many mind?"

Nobutada tries again to explain: "You have mind sword, mind people watch, mind enemy. Too many mind. Must have no mind."

Something in the Samurai's advice clicks for Algren and he understands—even if just a little. He repeats the concept back to Nobutada: "No mind."

Throughout the next sequence of sparring scenes, you see how Algren's swordsmanship improves, and his understanding of mushin and attention begins settling in, until he stops thinking so much that he defeats Nobutada.

Beginner's Mind

Beginner's mind is a Zen concept (also used in martial arts training) that says if you want to learn anything well, you must attain the plain and simple attention of an infant, whose mind is empty and fresh. It has no preconceived ideas. It sees things as they are. It is free from the habits of experience and therefore open to all possibilities. Cruise's character, Algren, exhibits beginner's mind when the idea of mushin and its link to attention clicks. What's important is that, as alien as the concept is to him, he never stops entertaining it. And eventually he understands.

Beginner's mind sounds a lot like mushin, and is reminiscent of Isabella's mindset that morning in the kitchen. But it is not the same as either. An infant's mind is like a sac of clear, vibrant attention without any derivatives. Pure and alert, this is the awareness with which we are born. Mushin, on the other hand, is a tool in our attention toolbox. It helps us rinse our slate clean again so that we can drop into beginner's mind whenever necessary. By the time a person reaches my daughter's age of 3, the need is already there and only increases from that point on. This brings us back to J.D. Salinger, who says that by our late teens our attention may not even be ours anymore. And what makes things even trickier is that we are probably unconscious of the loss. As it turns out, today's psychologists and neurologists agree.

Focus/Execute—Rinse/Repeat

As early as 1951, the well-known physicist David Bohm defined *attention* as a control *skill* we all need in order to manage outcomes in our life. Bohm emphasized that, like all skills, attention develops incrementally and continues to develop throughout your lifetime. For this reason, your attention isn't perfect all the time. In fact, said Bohm, it is common to experience some uncertainty creeping into your attention as you maneuver toward daily goals.

The problem is that uncertainty creates hesitation, and hesitation pulls you into a tangle of thoughts to try to clear the confusion. Consistent with martial arts teaching, Bohm explained that as you concentrate on any single thought, the full range of your attention starts to decay (distort). Thus, you can no longer link your thought to the largest number of options. And this is fine if you have already identified what is best for you at the moment—you're thirsty, there is a water fountain you have used before, the water is good, and so you think, "I'll sip some water from that fountain." Your solution works. But say you're driving in an unfamiliar city and looking for a good restaurant. You spot one—not your happiest choice, but acceptable. The restaurant is off the main highway, and you are not sure how to get there. You concentrate on looking for the right crossroad. You find your way and end up eating at the restaurant. The next day you spot what would have been your first choice—ironically on the other side of the street from where you initially saw the one you selected. Had you shifted your attention, even for a moment, you would have seen it. Your sequence of actions got you dinner, but didn't achieve the most desired results. Students experience the same phenomenon when they answer a test question one way and then later, upon reflection, see that there were several better options they could have chosen. Consider this scenario: A pet dog bee-lines across the street to get to something on the other side. It is so focused on what it wants that it fails to see an oncoming vehicle. This time, the decay of attention is catastrophic.

It almost seems as if nature has forced us to choose between having a sharp thought in place of seeing the big picture, and seeing the big picture instead of having a sharp thought. Doesn't seem like much of a choice. Imagine having to pick between switching lanes on the Interstate during rush hour with clear vision of the vehicle next to you, while losing sight of all else; or having clear vision of all other traffic, with no sight of the car next to yours. Again, not much of a choice. Considering the amount of mental data needed for a procedure such as switching lanes, it's amazing that we can execute the maneuver at all. Nonetheless, we do—and usually quite well. But remember all of the uncertainty the first time you tried it?

Martial arts teach that toggling your attention from the big picture to a narrower one is natural, necessary, and doesn't have to be a problem. *Focus/execute* is the term used in martial arts training to describe the sequence when it is done right: you focus on a specific task, execute it, rinse (empty your mind), and move on to the next task. Your mind learns naturally to flow from wide open to tight. And eventually, with enough repetition, you will make this process automatic. If not, the swordsman will wind up on his back for taking an irresistible swipe of the blade at the wrong time— or, off the mats, you may wind up side-swiping the car next to you by not overriding your immediate urge to switch lanes at just that time. This is where mushin plays in.

Mushin helps you toggle through focus/execute settings like clockwork, without the usual snags of uncertainty and confusion. It enhances your natural ability to prevent incoming data from quickly adding up to information overload, or your mind from temptingly sticking to any one piece of information. It keeps your focus calm and lucid up to the point of execution.

The Big Question

"How do you reach mushin?" I asked my sensei.

"That's the big question," he said.

He tapped me on the shoulder and motioned me to the center of the room. This was his way of answering most of my questions.

I positioned myself in a fighting stance, and we began a light spar. From the get-go, I was having trouble holding my focus. I felt anxious. My attention jumped from one thing to another, and I had this overwhelming urge to do something, anything. So I began throwing strikes. In fact, I was throwing almost all of the strikes. My teacher, on the other hand, was doing almost nothing. When he did throw a strike, it hit. I rationalized that all of his training had made him a faster puncher. But eventually I would discover that he had trained his *mind* to be faster, which is what made all the difference. I had a lot to learn.

Getting tagged—often—was usual for me in those early days. I had yet to learn that true speed comes from the way you mentally process information and from correct decision-making, not just the urge to do things fast.

Once while sparring a more advanced student, I saw my instructor watching from the other side of the dojo. All I could think about was how I would love to nail my opponent, just this once, and impress my teacher. I concentrated my effort and tried to make it happen by launching a showy cartwheel kick at my partner. But she easily blocked it. Then she swept my feet from under me, landing me face-down on the mats.

My instructor wasn't impressed—at least, not with me. Instead, he switched places with her and asked me to stay out on the mats. "I want you to see something," he said.

We moved to the center of the room, and the lesson began. All of his movements were soft and easy. His eyes were wide and deep like a cat's; they seemed like mirrors—completely attentive, yet unthinking. This is what many refer to as the martial arts stare.

My job was to journey into those mirrors and learn something about paying attention.

I had the sensation that my teacher could predict every move I was going to make. In coming years, I would learn that science would say we are all capable of making such predictions. In fact, our brains are wired so that we can—and at incredibly fast speeds. But, for me, understanding that capability, not to mention using it, was still a ways off.

"This is the kind of mental intensity you want," my sensei commented.

When I had been sparring earlier, the intensity I'd shown was the kind of grunting, growling aggression you'd use to chop wood. That kind of concentrated focus is pure *in*tention. What he was trying to show me was the opposite: *at*tention.

"Be patient," he said. "Try to see your target instead of think about it."

I was beginning to realize that I had been missing the real targets a lot. It occurred to me that intention without good attention could be outright dangerous.

"One single thought is all it takes to create an interval in your actions. That's when you're most likely to make a mistake and are incapable of acting fast enough to correct it," he added.

The Japanese call this dangerous interval (interruption of thought) *suki*. The best thing to do if suki happens is accept it—whatever you do, don't resist, or the interval will only intensify, creating the tangle of thoughts and uncertainty Bohm was talking about.

To help me understand, my teacher gave me an image. "Let your mind flow like water," he said. "Whenever you have a thought, let it float across the surface of your mind like a reflection, uninterrupted. If you practice this, your mind can become so quick it will appear automatic." He never mentioned physics to me, yet he and David Bohm were surely on the same page.

"Now do you understand?" he asked.

I understood intellectually, but it would be a while before I really got it.

In the days and months ahead, he never argued his point about attention. The mats would *show* me. He knew that. Then, after many more months of sparring, a higher-ranked student and I were going at it with our teacher watching. The senior student tagged me with a sequence of kicks and then launched a fast straight punch at my head. Without thinking, I raised my arm to block the strike, turned, and executed a counter strike. This all happened in an instant.

"Very good!" commented my sensei. "Perfect, and you didn't even think about it."

This was perhaps one of my earliest experiences at feeling mushin. I was starting to let my mind flow instead of interrupting it with damaging thoughts about what I should or shouldn't be doing. Practice and experience were paying off.

Okay, Let's Tear Attention Apart

As I stepped outside the world of martial arts and journeyed into the realm of science, I found my way to the office of Dr. Tram Neill, a leading psychologist at the University of Albany.[1] I had first come across Neill's work in the *McGraw-Hill Yearbook of Science and Technology*, for which he had written a chapter on perception.[2] I then went on to discover the plethora of research he had conducted on the topic, referenced by attention scientists seemingly everywhere.

What had attracted me to his work were his extensive studies in the area of *selective attention*; that is, your brain's ability to choose, moment by moment, what information is pertinent to your immediate goals—and what information is not. It was my hope that the more detailed picture he might share about what is happening inside the brain when you simply stop thinking and pay attention would help me fine-tune the system of attention skills my sensei had taught me decades ago.

Dr. Neill's office looked like what you might expect a research scientist's "pad" to look like: tall bookcases packed with books, stacks of paperwork everywhere, a desktop computer in the center of a large desk, more paperwork surrounding that, and a couple of chairs with more loaded bookshelves and mounds of paperwork around them. There were diagrams of the human brain on the wall and a large research laboratory right next door. I had waited a little over a week to speak with him and was quite excited to begin.

"So where do we start?" he asked.

Neill settled into his chair. He is soft-spoken and relaxed, dresses in flannel shirts and jeans in winter, and is easy to speak with. His research, which I have come to admire, holds many clues to help decode the mysteries of human attention.

I began by sharing Isabella's take on "brain science" with him, and a huge smile erupted across his face. I noticed some framed pictures of his children above a sidewall bookcase. *Perhaps Isabella's remark had reminded him of something his own children may have once said*, I thought.

His response came in the form of a question: "If, in 200 years, science could replace a single neuron in your brain with a transistorized neuron that is exact in every way, would your mind still be yours?"

"I believe it would," I answered. "You'd still have the same information in your head; your memories, and feelings, they would all still be there, no?"

"That's right," he said. "Now what if you replaced *all* of your neurons with transistors; would your mind still be yours?"

There is a difference between what Neill calls *form* (the actual cells that make up your brain) and *content* (what information you put in and out of your brain). "Content *is* your mind," he said.

This difference is at the heart of understanding what attention is and how you can use it effectively. It is also at the heart of Isabella's determination to keep her attention her own.

Neill insists your mind is a composite of data (information) that has entered it, *and* what you do with that data. In Neill's explanation, similar to Bohm's, your attention plays a part in the process.

He explained that at that very moment, parts of our minds were to some extent the same—that is, we were sharing similar information. (I immediately thought of two different computers downloading some of the same data, or having a few bags of the same groceries in our shopping carts and then going home and doing our own thing with the items.) But what we were doing with that data was different. The point is that even though you share your attention with other people (other minds), in the end, what you do with the information you take in can be as uniquely yours as a fingerprint.

In this sense, Isabella's off-the-cuff comment about her attention being "hers" was amusingly quite accurate and something many researchers with whom I have spoken say is worth noting, especially in terms of maintaining good attention when we become adults.

When I spoke with Neill's colleague, psychologist Frank Vellutino, director of the Child Research and Study Center at the University at Albany, he pointed out that Isabella was at a stage of development that we all must go through.[3] Hearing that was, in a way, a disappointment. I had heard the stories about how Einstein literally had an extra section in his brain that ordinary people like me do not and how this was at least partially responsible for his genius. The proud father in me fantasized hearing that my daughter might potentially have extraordinary gray matter as well. But Dr. Vellutino explained, "We all go through a phase when we see things in the possessive—as literally belonging to us."

"Even our mind?" I asked.

"Even our mind," he said. "It's all about control and ownership."

And this, it turns out, is good—and vital as we move on into adulthood. Feeling ownership of your own mind gives you a sense of control of your life. Neill explained that ownership generates confidence and helps build a positive world view. As such, feeling as though you are *not* in control can lower self-esteem and can create other problems as well, such as depression. Both of these conditions slow thinking even further and make you feel inauthentic. Going back to *The Catcher in the Rye*, Salinger was trying to convince us that maintaining ownership of your mind is not easy, but is imperative if your thoughts are ever going to feel authentic and effective. But is this easier said than done?

Developing a strong awareness of self, or your ability to feel and own what's in your mind (content), can be a good first step, and developing empathy, or your ability to feel what other people are feeling (their content), can be your next.

"Empathy has a lot to do with getting and maintaining control," explained Vellutino.

By letting other people's feelings into your field, you can see and consider how your behavior affects others. Empathy enables you to predict the consequences of your actions. It is a vital growth step because it provides you more information with which to gauge your responses as you work toward daily goals. For example, if you know your partner tunes out whenever you raise your voice, even though you only do it for emphasis, you can choose a more mutually successful way to emphasize things.

For those of us without extra brain matter like Einstein, what becomes extraordinary in our lives is what we do with the data we gather—what unique procedures we create and utilize in our day-to-day routines. And this is where possessiveness and empathy can really play into the mix.

Dr. Todd Wysocki, a colleague and friend, suggests that the kind of possessiveness Isabella demonstrated was more than just words. "It's about *self*, who you are and what you are feeling on the inside," he says.[4] And according to Wysocki, once your mind is connected to others and shares content, you are able to predict how what you do affects them and how what they do affects you. Your sense of self helps you aim your attention where it will do the most good, aligning your needs with your actions and with the needs and responses of others. The more self-aware you are, the more effective and genuine your actions can become. Feeling real gives you a sense of being more in control as well as better life management skills. Confidence and positiveness follow naturally. And your attention, just like your body, matures.

On the other hand, poor self-awareness can be pretty hazardous. An interesting example can be taken from the work of iconic psychologist B.F. Skinner. In his famous Skinner box study, which he developed to examine animal behavior, an animal is typically placed in a box that contains a lever and a green light in the front. The animal learns that if it pushes the lever when the green light flashes, it will receive a reward.

Neill explained, "Let's say I put you and a rat into a Skinner box. Every time the green light flashes and you push the lever, you get a dollar. Every time the rat pushes the lever, it gets Purina Rat Chow (There really is a "Purina Rat Chow"). We both laughed. The point was that we could conduct the test a thousand times until the response was fully conditioned. And I imagined this rat holding his own pretty well against me. I was amused. "By then, the rat's behavior would be pretty well set," I remarked.

Neill arched his eyebrows. He leaned back in his chair and said, "But let's say I took you aside and told you that I was going to install a red light in the box, and that if you push the bar when the red goes on, you will receive a lethal electrical shock. You wouldn't push the bar."

The rat, on the other hand, unfortunately would. "But," Neill commented, "don't feel too bad for the rat. Rats can usually get by just living with their own conditioning."

One thing that makes us different from not only rats but other animals as well is our ability to create, with our mind, events that haven't happened. We, as opposed to other creatures, can attend imagined scenarios and have feelings and thoughts about them, consider a variety of probabilities, and then, all things considered, "think about" and decide how we want our experiences to go. Here, thinking helps you see how to get the job done—how to attend. It helps you connect what happens to you (your self) with your desires, and helps you make choices. It helps you feel in control.

Similar to my sensei, Neill also emphasized that no one is telling you not to think. "It's all related: attention, organizing ways to get what you need, and thinking," he said.

During the 1960s, according to Neill, scientists liked comparing the mind to a computer. However, the idea of a single computer controlling everything you do has been replaced with an image of several computers that control specific parts of your brain. These areas include things such as language, motor skills, pleasure, pain, and emotions. Each area can be seen as its own computer filled with its own specific data, and each reports to your attention's CEO, which can decide what is relevant and what is not, what you respond to, as well as how, when, and why.

Neill explained there are two types of information that we pay attention to and store in our brain: The first is called *declarative knowledge* and the other is *procedural.* "In common language," he explained, "the distinction is made most clearly by whether we say 'knowing THAT' or 'knowing HOW.' Whereas declarative knowledge is propositional—has a truth value—procedural knowledge consists of the skills and operations we apply to declarative knowledge."

As such, procedural knowledge doesn't have a clear true or false. It varies in degree. "You learn 'how' to ride a bicycle," Neill explained, "but there is no point at which riding a bicycle is true or false."

On the other hand, I know that my mother's middle name was Veronica—declarative—and I know how to write my mother's middle name down and count the number of letters it contains—procedural.

When you sit down and have a conversation with your partner or a friend, you only rely on a tiny amount of all the truths you know. Procedural (skill) knowledge, on the other hand, can be activated moment-by-moment to help you reach your goals.

Here's another way to look at it: Procedural knowledge is taking what you know (declarative knowledge) and doing something with it, such as alphabetizing the following list of last names:

- Smith
- Jones
- Lee
- Heathe

Try it. See if you can feel the procedure for alphabetizing kicking in to do the job. Notice how quickly it engages.

Can you imagine life without the capacity for storing and recalling these virtually automatic procedures? You would have to re-learn even basic operations every time you need them—holding a fork, walking, talking, and even writing your name. Suffice it to say, we use and rely on procedural information a lot more often in our daily lives than declarative. And this is good, as long as the procedures we have stored are getting us what we want. They provide high-speed solutions to daily life management, and reduce our need to think. This frees up brain space and as a result quickens our thinking power for other tasks, including reflecting or analyzing.

Psychologists define attention as what (data) you are putting into your working memory to activate procedures to achieve immediate goals.

In an uncanny way, your field of attention operates like an ultra-sophisticated fetching system, targeting a piece of declarative information, bringing it into your memory, and connecting it to other information you have placed there to create processes you use to accomplish your needs. For example: You know THAT you are hungry. You know THAT there is a pizza place around the corner. You know HOW to get to the pizza joint. You know HOW to order pizza. You know HOW to eat it without making too much of a mess.

Attention's Chain of Command

Let's take a closer look. Psychologists say that attention isn't exactly a single switch you turn on or off. Instead it is made up of several switches that control a chain of components. Part of having good attention is turning on the right link in the chain, in the right amount, at the right time. And even a little knowledge about how each component works goes a long way, especially in helping identify what's working well in your attention toolbox as opposed to what's not pulling its weight.

This view of attention helps explain why it is possible for you to excel in one area of attending and not in another. For example, you can have really weak listening skills—you can't remember someone's name a minute after hearing it—but you can have off-the-charts visual attention—you might be able to recall the color of someone's eyes after only talking to that person for just seconds.

There are several component models of attention with considerable overlap. Most include similar links; however, the language used to describe these links and the number of links in the chain may differ. As such, I have taken the liberty to combine several of these models in order to provide the widest possible picture and to establish a uniformity of language with other sections of this book.[5]

In short, the first component is known as *focused attention*: your ability to focus on sensory data—what you see, hear, touch, smell, and taste. Psychologists say that it is common for us to be better tuned in to one of these than to another. As previously mentioned, a person may have great visual attention, yet is unable to listen very well.

Sustained attention is the next component. This refers to your ability to stay focused on any one thing. The opposite of good sustain is a feeling of being scattered or the feeling that your mind is wandering. Psychologists tell us that maximum sustain is only about 10 minutes. After that, your attention begins to fade. The good news, however, is that the fix is often as simple as reopening or widening your focus and letting it breathe, so to speak, even if just for a moment.

Selective attention is your ability to shut things out of your field of focus—to selectively concentrate on one aspect of incoming sensory data and ignore others. Psychologists say that at any given point you are so flooded with data that if you paid attention to all of it, you would be so overwhelmed that your other processing abilities, such as speech, spatial awareness, and thought would start to shut down. To help, nature has endowed us with the inborn capacity to narrow our attention to a tiny fraction of incoming data, as well as toggle back and forth between them. Your ability to carry on a conversation in a noisy room is a good example. Neill called this ability the Cocktail Party Effect. We've all experienced it—you're at a party with dozens of conversations going on, yet you are still able to listen carefully to what a friend is saying while ignoring other conversations going on in the same space.

Alternating attention comes next. According to researchers, attention isn't usually about just focusing on a single piece of sensory data or one task and keeping your focus there. It is more often about toggling from one task to another and from one piece of incoming information to another. The proverbial three-way conversation offers a good example: If your home is anything like mine you may, at times, find yourself in the middle of a phone call and someone in the room with you is dictating information he or she wants you to relay to the person on the other end of the line. *Encoding*, which is your brain's ability to get data into working memory storage, helps you to put your attention on what one person is saying, store it, and go back to your conversation with another person, melding the two.

Attention's CEO is known as *executive attention*. This link is all about choice. Importantly, it has the split-second ability to override impulses and attractions for more favorable understated options. It is what takes over when the mother hustling to strap three screaming toddlers into their car seats so she can load groceries into her car notices, in an instant, that one of the children has unstrapped and is running out into traffic. It is the driver heading through a green light who, in a split second, avoids hitting a dog that has strayed into her path. It is the martial artist who avoids an opportunity to show off in place of making the right move. It is the employee who on a Friday afternoon avoids an argument and instead goes home light, happy, and secure.

The Deer in the Headlights

Despite your attention's capacity to veto impulses for better options, seeing and processing information takes time and effort, according to psychology and psychiatry professor Richard Davidson of the University of Wisconsin School of Medicine.[6]

Seeming to trail what Bohm opened up in the 1950s, Davidson explains that we only have so much brain power. Paying close attention to one thing—by either thinking or narrowing our focus for too long—may mean the tradeoff of missing what information follows shortly thereafter.

"When your attention gets stuck on the first target," says Davidson, "you miss the second one. This effect is called 'attentional blink,' as when you blink your eyes, you are briefly [momentarily] unaware of visual signals."[7] Consequently, your attention temporarily shuts down. The potential problem is that the next detail may just be the one you want or need most.

Professor Joel Warm, of the University of Cincinnati, also talks about distractions and how they break your attention. Warm reports, "the phenomenon is that the more you look, the less you see."[8] This brings us back to *suki* or an interrupting thought, which, remember, in martial arts is overcome with empty mind.

I recently questioned a literature student, "Do you see any similarities between Stephen King and Edgar Allen Poe?" The student started to answer by referencing King's latest novel, but got bogged down when he couldn't remember the title. You could see he felt stuck. There was a slightly noticeable edge to him—he talked a little faster, seemed to move a little more jaggedly, and lost focus. His energy surged and was heading for overdrive. His insistence on remembering the title interrupted him, and in the end, he completely lost track of the question. In fact, he asked if I would repeat it. His attention had been invaded by a sideline detail and that detail completely took over. Similar things happen to all of us, all the time.

Neill showed me just how easily my focus could be grabbed by an unexpected detail. He asked me to look at a group of random letters scattered across a white page. This seemed simple enough. The letters were the same size, and they all, except for one, were black. On the outside, right edge of the group, was one red letter. My eyes immediately stopped on the red one, and so did my mind. It was as if I had no choice. I could feel my "open focus" narrow down and tighten onto the one red letter. Neill explained that this is what can happen when an "unusual" detail enters your field of attention.

For me, the effect was immediate. And whether this is good or not depends on the circumstances. For the mother loading groceries into her car and noticing that her child is about to run into traffic, this "invasion" of detail is a good thing. For the student so tightly focused on remembering the title of Stephen King's last novel and losing sight of the bigger question—not so good. Neill's demonstration had shown me firsthand how incidents such as this can stop your attention dead—as he put it, "Like a deer caught in headlights."

On the flip side, Davidson's research, as well as others, maintains that our ability to sometimes catch a second signal even though we are cued in on the first is possible with the proper mental control. Furthermore, gating your attentional links and developing a strong awareness of self and empathy can help you manage and generate speedier and more accurate procedures. They also help you attend in ways that will increase your levels of success for both your immediate and long-term goals.

The question, then, is how do we do it? The answer brings us back to the pre-dawn of martial arts; in fact, millennia ago, high into the Sung Mountains of China.

China, A.D. 525

Martial arts began with the development of language itself and can be traced back over 3,000 years in China. It wasn't, however, until thousands of years later that these combat disciplines fused with philosophy, when in A.D. 525 Buddhist monk Bodidharma trekked across the Himalayas from India to the ancient Shaolin Temple, located high in the thick, pine forests of China's Sung Mountains. What he found was that the monks who lived and worked there were deficient, both mentally, in that they lacked vigor and attentiveness, and physically, in that they could not defend themselves against assailants. These vulnerabilities disturbed him greatly. Consequently, he taught them a regimen of attention-building exercises including deep breathing, mushin, and meditation. He also included into the monks' daily routines a regimen of exercises taken from the movements of animals. In time, the combination of all these activities evolved into what is now known as Kung Fu. Many believe, to this day, that Kung Fu is the core of all martial arts as we presently know them. Bodidharma's teachings piloted martial arts from a one-dimensional exploration of combat into a holistic discipline for the strengthening of mind and body.

By the mid-19th century, when the need for fighting skills in the Orient diminished, martial training emphasized personal and mental development: living a better life, becoming a better parent, friend, and human being. Combat maxims were replaced with ideals of self-awareness and welfare, along with axioms such as: *empty your mind*; *truth comes between breaths (or "thoughts")*; *maximum benefit with minimum effort (or stressors)*; *cultivate an alert mind*; *let your mind flow.* Martial arts became more about improving your mind and inner self than about fighting—all in the hope of creating a better, freer, longer life, with the possibility of enlightenment. From this point on, attention skills were placed at the center of one's training. Self-awareness became an ultimate goal. And at the heart of all mind-enhancing exercises was meditation.

On the Other Side of History: The Presidential Election of 2008

Picture a device that looks like a shower cap and is packed with enough electrodes to throw a 3D digital image of your brain on a high-definition monitor. Not only that, but it can measure your thoughts and feelings at speeds better than one-six-hundred-thousandth of a second—seems a far cry from meditation, but is it? The instrument I have described is used by a new neuroscience that is so precise it can catch you thinking about your hair, even when you insist that you are in truth paying serious attention to what someone is saying. You might be thinking, okay, been there, done that—in fact, often. Ditto for your author. But why do we say one thing when we are feeling something else? Are we lying? Or are we just not paying attention—to ourselves? Moreover, is there anything we can do about the discrepancy that can improve our overall thinking power?

Dr. Fernando Miranda is chief science director for a West Coast company called Lucid Systems. Lucid's expertise is generating cutting-edge scientific research for marketing/advertising development. By trade, Dr. Miranda is a neurophysiologist and surgeon as well as a former faculty member at Johns Hopkins School of Medicine. His teammates at Lucid are all heavyweights in the neuroworld, with credentials in neurosurgery, neuron imaging, neurological disorders and rehabilitation, and thousands of pages of research into what and how people think. Lucid Systems specializes in what catches and guides people's attention, the kind of information that makes pollsters and advertisers drool.

What brought me to Dr. Miranda's work was a fascinating story that rocketed across major media networks. Covered on CNN, ABC's *Today* show, Discovery, and featured in the *Wall Street Journal*, the story demonstrated beyond doubt that Lucid Systems knew exactly how to catch people's attention.

Picture this: It's January 7, 2008, the day before the all-important New Hampshire Presidential Primary. You have been watching Clinton, Obama, and Edwards duke it out for weeks on the Democratic side, and Republicans McCain, Romney, Huckabee, Giuliani, and Paul on the other side. You may have wondered, at times, if people would really go to the voting booth and pull the lever for a woman or for an African American. Would conservatives say yes to a Republican who had been tagged as too liberal by his colleagues? Nearly every television broadcast you have seen covering the elections has displayed charts that track undecided voters' attention moment by moment, measuring their approval, disapproval, and what they like and dislike about the candidates. Perhaps you have wondered about the accuracy of these charts.

Then, on the day before the New Hampshire Primary, the *Today Show* headlines a story that cites the millions of dollars political campaigns spend on polls. Katie Couric smiles, saying that people not only lie to pollsters but to themselves. She teases, saying that when some people say they're thinking about politics, they're really thinking about somebody's hair.

The segment is a piece on how cutting-edge neuroimaging is able to reveal the truth about your thoughts and feelings, as well as about what you are or are not paying attention to. A picture comes up on the television screen and shows a person's brain on politics. The imaging looks uncannily like Doppler radar, only in color. The back of the brain on screen is clouded red, indicating what is being referred to as "pure unadulterated feeling." The color red shows that the person likes what he or she is feeling.

Couric's story centers on an experiment conducted by Lucid Systems and Dr. Miranda. Guinea pigs for the experiment are a group of "undecided" New Hampshire voters watching the ABC debate and trying to decide who they like best. The group watches as Hillary Clinton gets emotionally worked up: "I want to make change," she says emphatically, "but I've already made change." She is referring to herself as the first woman running for the office of President. Then she gets a little silly, pretending to be sad (facial expressions and all) about the questioner's not having noticed. She smiles. Lucid System's electronic scans show that the group likes her responses very much.

But when Barack Obama comes back, saying not to worry, that she is already "likable enough," scans show a huge negative response among group members. "The voters aren't even aware of how much they don't like the comment," a Lucid representative says. Their attention has been turned off. Self-awareness (or in this case a lack of) plays in when later the group is asked to dig deeper and reflect into why they didn't like Obama's remark. Group members make comments such as, "Barack was ruining her fun," and "He just doesn't like her very much," and that bothered them. Another surprise, the group praises Edwards for many of his comments, yet flat-lines on the screens; truth be told, they aren't emotionally moved. Again, their attention has been turned off to what they are actually feeling in favor of something else. Later, when asked to reflect on that discrepancy, group members explain they don't think Edwards could back up his many inflated statements.

Nonetheless, the *USA Today* Gallop Poll gave Obama the lead—straight into primary night. But one day later, New Hampshire voters gave Clinton their vote. So where did the polls go wrong? Are pollsters missing what people's brains are actually saying? Or is the discrepancy a byproduct of someone's poor attention? If so, whose?

Dr. Miranda uses electrode-loaded instruments that measure perspiration and muscle movement—emotional reactions that track your attention and show what you really like or dislike. And sometimes, he notes, we really do say what we are feeling. But what's happening when there are discrepancies like those indicated in the New Hampshire experiment? Are we lying? Dave Remer, cofounder of Lucid Systems, describes it as "more of an unarticulated truth."

Miranda explains, "As we grow older, we learn to be politically correct. All of the unspoken layers that come with this cover up the unspoken truth."[9]

You turn away from your true feelings (your self-awareness) by putting your attention elsewhere—in this case, on political correctness. For example, Lucid interviewed a white voter who insisted he liked McCain and Obama equally, but scans showed he really liked Obama more. On the other hand, they interviewed an African American male who criticized Clinton, saying, "She kind of embodies the old school of politics," but whose brain showed he really did like what she said.

"It all has to do with what you are pumping down into your field of attention," Miranda told me. "There are 11 million bits of data flowing through your brain per second. But you can only handle about 40. Right now you are receiving millions of data on the status of your right toe."

The "thought" amused me. As if a magnet had pulled my thoughts there, I immediately started thinking about my toe, warm and cozy inside my shoe; I could feel my sock around it, the bottom of my shoe beneath it, the floor, and so on. Miranda added, "But you weren't even thinking about your toe at all before I mentioned it." We shared a chuckle because we both knew I was undeniably thinking about it now.

"So," he explained, "You can shift your attention, turn components on and turn others off. You are like an orchestra director. You call in the violins, woodwinds, brass, percussion, and so on. You bring them in or not, slightly or intensely."

How much sensory data you pump in or out is called *gating*. Miranda brought his voice down to the slightest whisper. I immediately responded by perking my ears. It seemed to be an automatic reaction. "If I bring my voice down far enough, you will adjust," he said. This was because I automatically put my attention on my brain's audio center and turned up the volume. Most of our attention processes are unconscious because they happen so fast—within one-six-hundred-thousandth of a second, Miranda explained. And this, it turns out, is nature's way of protecting us: Perhaps the most well-known high-speed process we all come equipped with is fight-or-flight perception.

"You don't get to think about how fast you are going to run away from a dinosaur; you really have to just do it," Miranda said.

"But what happens when unconscious, high-speed perception is wrong? It seems to me this can get you into high-speed trouble," I commented.

"That's right," he said. "There is a story I use to illustrate the point." This was his version of Dr. Neill's "deer in the headlights" concept. Miranda continued.

"A man is being chased by a tiger. He runs through the woods very attentively. His entire attention is open and alert to the tiger potentially coming out from anywhere. Suddenly, out of the corner of his eye, he sees a rabbit. He can't help but to put his attention on the rabbit. It's not the tiger, but the man looks anyway. He has no choice."

"Pretty dangerous," I say.

"Yes," Miranda agreed. "Very."

I detailed the "test" I had participated in with Neill, and especially how the one odd letter in the group was capable of freezing my attention almost instantly. Miranda told me that such reactions can be accurately measured and occur in virtually milliseconds—and so you have a feeling of having no choice in the matter.

"When I walk into a room," he explained, "you see a Latino guy who is short and speaks with an accent. You go to your mental folder and categorize this data with what you've seen and experienced before and decide whether you like this person or not. In that 600,000th of a second, you have made up your mind. To change your mind after is difficult. In fact, it is an uphill battle, and lasts inordinately."

Too often, we just resign ourselves to such ultra-fast reactions, regardless of whether they are in our best interests or in our interests at all. But must we? Can we change processes that happen so fast we aren't aware of them?

"It's not easy. You have to flood your mind with new data," said Miranda. You have to create new processes that will trigger at the same high speeds. This brings us back to Neill's explanation of using incoming data to create new procedures.

According to Miranda, even though we are unconscious of such split-second perceptions, we *can* reflect on them. And reflection is an essential step in gaining control of high-speed thoughts and reactions—just as participants in the New Hampshire Primary experiment were able to learn something about their true feelings when discrepancies were brought to their attention via electronic instruments. Reflection makes it possible to fix existing procedures or replace them with new ones that are better aimed toward your current goals.

Martial arts do not rely on the electronics of the neuroworld. They do, however, emphasize the use of reflection—first, to "check in" with your self, and then to edit procedures so they are in synch with your goals. And I cannot overemphasize this notion of coordinating things you are attending to with the workings, conditions, and desires of your inner-most self. In fact, martial way insists on this. Additionally martial arts have historically taught that the best path to such reflection is meditation, and many psychologists and neurologists concur. In fact, there is a lot of research out there citing meditation as a viable nonmedical way to gain effective control over high-speed attentional processes that can disengage us from our true feelings.

If there is a smoking gun that emerges from this corroboration of science and ancient arts, it is this: There is now scientific proof that the regimen of mushin, focus/execute, meditation, and visualization skills works. And with this comes an even more user-friendly understanding of why these skills work, as well as how to use them to develop, edit, and even short-circuit a wide range of high-speed procedures to facilitate faster, sharper thinking upon command. What's more, high levels of self-awareness and empathy can help keep such procedures accurate and authentic.

Miranda noted that research on attention shows that brainwaves (electrical patterns in your brain) generated during meditation have the ability to slow down high-speed perceptions considerably. These brainwaves move your mind into a relaxed, alert level of awareness in which responses flow more naturally and more controllably. This slows down data entering your field of attention and allows you to attend to perceptions and procedures that would otherwise remain unconscious to you. Meditation allows you to toggle your attention between self, others, and the procedures you are firing as you work out your goals. Mountains of hard-wired laboratory research agree.

University of Pennsylvania neuroscientists Drs. Amishi Jha and Michael Baime report that "practicing even small doses of meditation can significantly improve people's attention, especially the ability to quickly and accurately focus as you manage tasks and prioritize goals."[10] What's significant about these findings is that they extended beyond just the improvement of alertness and into the improvement of other tasks. As Jha states it herself, "It's as if learning to ride a bike made you a better tightrope walker."[11]

Jha and Baime's findings have been echoed by the Waisman Laboratory for Brain Imaging and Behavior at the University of Wisconsin.[12] Similar results have also been found at Harvard, Yale, and M.I.T. These findings mount more evidence for what the ancients simply accepted as a necessary part of mental and physical training that dated back to Bodidharma and his teachings. Human attention is trainable and malleable. Skills such as mushin, focus/execute, meditation, and visualization have staying power. In fact, much good news in the neuroworld revolves around the notion of *plasticity*—that the brain can be changed. That our brains can be trained and changed is significant in terms of attention because it means that we are not doomed to a fixed allotment of alertness at birth that is ours for life. Indeed, it means the opposite. We now know that in as little as eight weeks, we, in many cases, can begin to reverse the toll that aging has on our attention. And according to many researchers, there is no ceiling to this improvement.

Does all this research suggest that there is something we can do to take control of feelings and thoughts that happen to us even when they occur in milliseconds? Can we learn to override discrepancies between what we say, what we think and feel, and what we do—as those seen in the 2008 Election Voter Polls? The answer is *yes*. If we take our power of attention seriously, there is a lot we can do to prevent those kinds of mistakes.

Let's Peek Inside the Meditating Brain

Imagine yourself sitting, eyes closed, with your attention on your breath or perhaps on a specific object in your environment. You are intentionally doing this to relax yourself and to get your mind off thinking. Whenever your attention wanders or thoughts predictably arise, you gently bring your attention back to your initial focus in order to bypass your urge to think. Doing so places your thought(s) in the background rather than the foreground of your attention.

This is the most common and popular form of attention meditation. It is often used to calm and de-stress the mind—and body—by putting you into a state of unthinking alertness. Research conducted at the W.M. Keck Laboratory emphasizes that with practice you can enter this state of mind at will even during daily routines—without the meditation itself. Remember how quickly the procedure for alphabetizing kicked in when you tried it? What made that possible was that you had, somewhere along the line, repeated the procedure enough to store it in your memory. Professor Davidson of the University of Wisconsin's School of Medicine says the same thing happens with the meditative mindset. For nearly the past two decades, Davidson has worked with the Dalai Lama, spiritual leader of Tibetan Buddhists, to study the effects of meditation at the Waisman Laboratory for Brain Imaging and Behavior.

"There is nothing mysterious about these activities," says Davidson. "They can be understood in terms of hard-nosed Western [science]."[13]

What's important is that meditation, according to Davidson, can be used to regulate attention and can be enhanced through learning.[14] Part of the learning experience is repetition and practice, and Davidson's studies show that this regimen eventually allows the process to trigger, upon command, without the meditation itself. This is huge if you are going to use your attentional mechanism to sharpen your thoughts, feelings, and responses to things.

There is another, perhaps less-common form of attention meditation. In this meditation, thought itself—in fact, your entire field of awareness—becomes the object of your attention. The first part of the meditation is identical to the previous one. The difference is that once you have quieted your mind, your job (for about 15 minutes) is to sit back and put your attention on the whole parade of thought flowing through your mind, without thinking about any of it. In a sense, you are training your attention's fetching system to become one of Dr. Miranda's electrode caps. You are, to all intents and purposes, scanning your own brain. You are peering into your *self*—the image that children such as Isabella are developmentally cued into for several years and that Salinger warns we run the risk of losing unless we grab on tightly.

According to Davidson, just the way physical exercise trains the body, attention skills can be trained and developed with practice.[15] Experiments conducted at the University of Pennsylvania show that even as little as 30 minutes of meditation daily can improve the ability to control attention and focus even for those with heavy daily demands.[16]

Let me give you one of these attention meditations so you can try for yourself. Don't worry if you make a mistake here or there.

Begin by opening your field of attention to its widest setting as in the first meditation in this chapter. Once you are calm and alert, focus on seeing and feeling what is emotionally happening in your body and mind, without interruption (suki). Notice any areas of tightness in your body (usually in the chest, shoulders, abdomen, and thighs) that begin to loosen. Let your mind relax even more. If scenes from incidents that have occurred in your life or ones you are imagining bubble up into your consciousness, just objectively watch them float by. These scenes may include people, places, things, events, feelings, and so on. Avoid any urge to grab onto any of these. Let your mind flow with these images, without any interference. Go wherever they lead; just keep going. Observe any procedures (yours and anyone else's who may enter into the field of your meditation) that seem to automatically engage. Notice the effects these procedures have on you and others, and especially on anyone's immediate goals.

Later, use your thinking power to reflect on and assess any automatic procedures you witnessed kicking in. Consider creating new procedures or tweaking already existing ones to help you better reach your goals.

This form of meditation uses your attention skills to merge your inside and outside worlds. It makes your responses to things faster, more self-aware, empathic, and effective. Thinking is minimized by placing it at the crossroads of experience and feeling wherein you create procedures and maneuver from them toward goals.

But you may be wondering just how and why meditation contributes to quick and crisp brain power. Science again helps provide an answer.

Remember that meditation allows you nonmedical access to brainwave patterns. Just a little background in the mechanics of these can help you understand the basics and relate them to your daily routines. First, all brainwaves are electrical movements in the brain. These movements can be measured using an electroencephalograph (EEG). Electrodes placed on the scalp measure the frequencies of these waves. From highest to lowest frequency, these brainwaves are called beta, alpha, theta, and delta.

Beta is your waking state, within which you think, listen, analyze and solve problems. This is your normal state of mind when at work, school, or shopping. Your attention generally starts out most alert, but the stressed-out feeling you get from one concentrated thought after another eventually dulls your attention, slows your thinking, and depletes your energy.

Alpha is slower. It makes you feel relaxed and reflecting and attentive of your surroundings. These waves bring about the relaxed, alert state of awareness that you experience during meditation. Alpha waves fuel creativity as well as generate faster, more decisive learning, without thinking.

Theta is even slower. It is the state between wakefulness and sleep. In this state, memories, thoughts, and other data that eludes you during your waking state can be recalled.

Your delta state is the slowest. This is the state in which deep, dreamless sleep occurs.

Brainwave levels not only provide insight into your mind, but they can also be stimulated to actually change your current level of awareness. By increasing or decreasing certain frequencies, you can move your attention through a variety of mental states that range from high alert to fully relaxed. Likewise, you can affect how intensely you enter each level.

Bodidharma didn't have access to instruments that could measure brain activity; nonetheless, what he was teaching the ancient monks, terminology notwithstanding, was that through meditation you can train your mind to enter a state of highly energized, clear, alpha lucidity at will—even within the slower theta state. Moreover, he taught them that the more you practice entering this state, the easier it gets to stay in it, and for longer periods of time. And as we proceed into the world of attention training, you will discover repetition is a practice with many virtues.

Today neurologists and psychologists have made significant breakthroughs in the study of how shifting modes naturally can allow people to enter states of increased intelligence, creativity, relaxation, and higher energy. At the cutting edge of such research is Dr. Siegfried Othmer, who insists that "Biofeedback is the attempt to train the body/mind to recover its natural self-regulatory capacity through a learning, or re-learning, process."[17] Othmer and his wife, Susan Othmer, are a husband-and-wife team who together founded the Othmer Institute, based in Hollywood, California. Practicing psychologists and pioneers of neurofeedback (EEG biofeedback, which uses electrodes to identify brainwave patterns), the Othmers have found that training brainwave shifts can generate "Improvements in IQ, calm the anxious mind, and return people to their friends and family—by helping people find the rhythms in their own brains."[18]

Othmer further reports that neurofeedback is a way of intervening on your body's attentional networks, memory, and specific cognitive function. It can help regulate moods, emotions, motor control, and your ability to attend to the sensory world.[19] As such, neurofeedback ramps up self-awareness, self-esteem, and self-expression.

Researchers Dr. E. Green and K.S. Ozawkie report that, "Experimentally, theta feedback and vipassana [meditation] lead to states of mindfulness that are so much alike that theta training might, without exaggeration, be called 'instrumental' vipassana."[20]

Changing modes of attention from high, relaxed alertness to low isn't something you are taught in school. But a neurofeedback clinician can sit you down in his or her office and with the click of a button drive your attention from the kind of high, edgy alertness you'd feel after a Starbucks double espresso drink to the classic spaced-out feeling you get when you stare at your cell phone wondering who it was you were about to call. Neurofeedback works to improve attention by using such instruments to help you feel each mode (beta, alpha, theta, delta) as it kicks in. As a result, you become more sensitive to how your body feels and reacts upon each shift and ultimately learn how to select appropriate levels of attention on your own, sans instrument, at will.

What's important is that you don't have to rely on people in white lab coats and machines to help you do this. You can learn to activate and toggle between the same modes of attention naturally—through meditation.

The whole electronics-versus-natural-skill argument will probably go on for a long time to come. It reminds me of a similar argument from the world of music: Many musicians consider Jimi Hendrix the first of the great "electric" guitarists. These people argue that Hendrix created many of the effects we hear in his music (as well as in today's music) with just the use of his fingers, guitar, and amplifier. I am one of these people. Still, I have nothing but admiration for the engineers who created electronic gadgets to reproduce Hendrix's effects. Their engineering allowed the rest of the guitar-playing world to sound like Hendrix, even though they may not have possessed his unique blend of skills in their fingertips. I'm all right with this interaction between art and science because it keeps raising the bar of human potential. Hendrix used and out-played every electronic device that came before him, and newcomers will use and out-play the electronics that have preceded them too.

Zen Breathing

Imagine that you have been enrolled in a martial-arts program for about a month. Your instructor has scheduled a class that is to meet before sunrise and you have agreed to participate. When the day finally arrives, it is a bone-chilling winter morning. It is snowing and everything outside is covered with ice. The sky is dark and the moon is still glowing—cold and pale. Snow has coated the glassy tree branches and power lines. The whole world is quiet and glistening and puffed white. Imagine heading out into this blistery air and delicious wintry scene pumped up with that adventurous feeling you get when you are about to do something a bit out of the ordinary.

You arrive at the dojo, and your instructor asks the dozen or so students who have gathered to sit in rows, cross-legged on the mats, facing the room's 20-foot-high windows. You notice that it is still dark out and snowing even harder than when you left your home. The room is cold and so are you. Your instructor sits in front of the group and tells you that today you are going to learn a new way of breathing. You are curious because so much about martial arts has already been about relearning and training basic skills, beginning with how to pay attention and now to breathing. Your instructor has two wooden blocks, one in each hand, resting across his legs.

"When I clap these blocks together," he says, "I want you to breathe in, filling your lungs with air. Use the bottom of your lungs to pull the air in. This will force you to breathe abdominally. Most people only use the top of their lungs, not the bottom, and therefore they do not take in enough air. I don't want you to exhale until you hear me hit it again, and so on."

There is a soft whooshing sound as everyone exhales together. Then the clack of the blocks and everyone inhales.

"Visualize the air you are breathing as clean, white fog coming in through your nose," your instructor says. "Then visualize it flowing through your whole body, charging it everywhere and then exiting through your mouth."

In concept, the breathing-in-and-out exercise is simple, yet in the beginning you feel it is a little difficult to keep in synch. You wonder if you are the only one feeling this way. You keep trying anyway. You gradually discover that visualizing your breath as fog flowing in and through your body has kept any other thoughts from entering your mind. You find that the longer you maintain this focus the more relaxed you get. The chill you felt earlier disappears and your body feels warm. Your mind feels light and sharp and ready to flow in any direction.

A few days later, the scene is quite different. You are running around your home feeling anxious because you can't remember where you put the car keys. What's more, you are concerned that you will be late for work. Your adrenaline is up and that's not helping. In fact, it is making you feel more anxious. Your mind flashes to the dojo. You remember how calm and good you felt after your breathing exercise. And so you shift. Instead of continuing the search for your keys, you pull back your concentration, and widen your focus—as if you were looking out the dojo windows again into the vast wintry scene outside. You relax and breathe the way your sensei taught you. This instantly makes you feel better, calmer. Because this feels right, you keep your focus as wide as possible. This makes you stop thinking about your keys. Suddenly an image of the keys pops into your mind, and you see where you left them. You are perfectly confident they are there—and they are. You are somewhat amazed that things can happen so easily. You head to work, trying to maintain the same clear, unfettered mind. You arrive on time, calm, confident, alert, and energized. You are keenly aware of having discovered a new way of working through a minor crisis. You already know you will use this method many more times again—especially before or during business meetings or confrontations.

Measured breathing, when combined with a meditative mindset, quickens and sharpens the mind. It restores calm, confidence, and strength. With repetition, you can learn how to use this technique anywhere and acquire its benefits on command.

Martial arts recommend combining measured breathing with any kind of physical activity. It is believed that this combination of activities boosts your production of positive energy and amplifies its effects. The practicing martial artist will use a variety of katas or exercise drills. But as one of my Kung Fu teachers once said, you can (and should) achieve the same effect by simply walking down the street. The point is that your body is a vessel that can only hold so much energy. When you combine measured, deep breathing with anything physical, you force low-quality energy out and replace it with new higher-quality energy. Any activity works, from katas to playing tennis, jogging, walking, gardening, or even housework. The effects of recharging, however, are only temporary. Therefore you must recharge often.

The Colonel

Sergeant Michael McLaren is a giant—6 feet, 7 inches tall—trained in 32 martial arts. He reminds me of a huge tree, with long, solid arms and long, powerful legs. Despite his size, he moves with speed and grace. He is agile enough to stand nose-to-nose with you and swing his leg over your head. Prior to our meeting, McLaren had been a Marine martial arts instructor in Okinawa, Japan, and it was he who introduced me to the Marine system of martial arts. Soon after, we became training partners and good friends.

Often after workouts, we would hang around the dojo, drinking bottled water and juices and talking. On one such occasion, our conversation turned to attention. "On the battlefield," he commented, "a loss of attention can make the difference between life and death. You have to be ready, for anything, and you have to execute fast and properly. You may not have a second chance."

Through McLaren, I learned that the U.S. Marine Corps considers good attention more than just good posture and a salute. In fact, the Corps has created a regimen of procedures to train attention skills. I became very curious about what these procedures were, and especially in what ordinary civilians could learn from them.

McLaren introduced me to Colonel Kevin Nally, commander of the U.S. Marine School in 29 Palms, California, the largest Marine base in the United States. Before taking over command at 29 Palms, Nally served as director of the Marine Corps Martial Arts Program (MCMAP). The attention skills and techniques in Nally's programs are used to help protect the lives of Marines all over the world.

Nally told me that mental acuity is of utmost concern in his program. "Equally important," he said, "a lot of our attention training emphasizes teamwork."[21]

He had touched a core principle of traditional martial art *bushido* (the samurai code of honor), which emphasizes that mental keenness and teamwork must go hand in hand. This brought me back to Dr. Valentino's insistence that empathy is necessary to mature our attention and successfully navigate toward goals. When I mentioned this to Nally, he remarked that "Everything you do affects everybody else around you and vice versa." For example, you can devise a way to get to the other side of a mountain, but it isn't much good if it puts the rest of your team at risk. I, for example, can respond to a student's question in the classroom until he or she is delighted, but my action isn't very effective if the exchange is detrimental to the rest of the class.

"There is another way to look at teamwork," explains Dr. Donald Ward.[22] Ward is an upstate New York biologist who has conducted extensive work in stem cell research at Rensselaer Polytechnic Institute (RPI). He is a good friend and mentor and lives in the same part of New York State as do my family and I. Hanging out in the woodlands surrounding our homes, we have shared a variety of discussions on the biology of attention. To Ward, human development begins at the cellular level—at the very brink of life. As he explains it, our first cells (stem cells) have the power to become anything they want, from an eye to a heart valve. They know what to do by paying attention to everything that is going on around them.

During development, cells are in constant communication with each other, working to determine what their roles will be as we mature as an organism.

"This process," Ward explains, "results in certain cells which create the strongest connections with their surrounding neighbors and microenvironment, becoming stronger and turning into the leaders or 'decision-makers.' At the same time, these controlling cells suppress this process from occurring in the neighboring cells and cause those secondary cells to take on supporting roles. Over time, this results in the creation of a nervous system with an architecture that is refined to function at a high level."

It amazed me how much the language concerning cell development related to the language of attention, and how many of the inner workings seemed parallel, particularly in ideas of self-awareness, teamwork, and some sense of self-regulation—in goal-achievement. From its earliest sparks, our nervous system knows to activate what's appropriate and inhibit what is not.

Ward insists that "This higher-level executive functioning is based on the integration of all the previous windows of development that have progressively built upon each other. Combine this nervous system with all the other systems of the body, and we observe the ultimate level of teamwork with many different cell types taking on different roles and performing different functions for the 'greater good' of the whole being."

Still talking cells and decision-making, Ward gives a dramatic example of what in attention training I would refer to as blocking information that is detrimental to an imminent goal or task: "When cells sustain genetic damage," Ward explains, "they perform the ultimate self-sacrifice for the overall good of the entire organism by committing suicide themselves instead of passing on this faulty DNA to other cells through cellular divisions."

As adults, we still have stem cells that are capable of going down different paths to become a range of varied cell types, depending on the microenvironment to which they are exposed and from which they gather specific signals or cues, and the communication the cells receive from the existing cells within that microenvironment. Ward calls this the "ready mode," meaning that within this state the cell is alert and prepared for anything; it can become anything. In order to make their move, these initial cells set their attention wide open, sense what needs to be done, and, using their internal capabilities, then just do it.

Nally's Marine Corps attention training is strikingly consistent with Ward's explanation of attention as it exists deep in our cells, traditional martial arts, psychology, neurology, neurofeedback, and meditation. Similar to all these disciplines, the MCMAP insists that attention begins with opening your mind's eye to its widest setting and cranking up your self-awareness and empathy to their highest, most sensitive levels. In fact, to drive the point home, the MCMAP motto reads, "One mind, any weapon." On the literal level, Nally says, this is to remind you that anything in combat can be turned into a weapon. Applied to daily life, however, he explains, it reminds you that you can draw on anything in your environment to help solve an imminent problem. "You have to pay attention to all of it without getting bogged down to any single detail as you flow from one goal to another."

Similar to all of the experts in this book, Colonel Nally emphasized the role of self-awareness and confidence in attention-building. What's important is that you simultaneously look (letting your empathy flow) inwardly (to self) and outwardly (to your environment) as you pick your actions. This keeps you focused on what's best for you and for everyone. Adding Ward's cell-talk to this, you can feel the power and etymology of self sparked into consciousness within our first tissues. When you consider the decision-making tasks necessary in order to attend to the building of an entire human body, I can't help but wonder how to consciously draw more of this power into our everyday lives.

Marine Corps instructors are trained to nurture confidence in their students whenever possible, during workouts and even during off-time—"it doesn't matter if you are in a field or a restaurant," Nally emphasized. Marines do this because confidence and self-awareness, according to the colonel, help make thoughts and actions more accurate. Martial arts, Zen, psychology, biology, and neuroscience agree.

But Nally adds a little something extra to the attention picture. When I asked him what he would say to someone who was fatigued or whose thinking was getting hazy, he said, "Think about the rest of your team; that's what I would say. Think about how your actions will affect them." Nally's point is that you can draw energy and alertness from empathetic thinking, more than you might imagine. My mind leapt to the story of a mother who couldn't swim, yet summoned the mental and physical capacity to rescue her drowning child, as well as to the plethora of stories involving empathy driven acts of heroism that called on skills way beyond a person's normal capacities.

Another unique exercise in attention training used in Nally's program is called "The Eight-Hour, Eight-Second Drill." This activity trains attention skills under extreme conditions. Imagine an eight-hour workout, including long-distance jogs, rock and mountain climbing, swimming, and the like, all in full military gear. Then, just as you approach the finish line, you find a dozen or so pumped-up Marines waiting to spar you—all-out, one-on-one—before you can really go home.

"In real life, conflicts don't just happen like they might in a dojo fight," explains Nally, "when you are rested up, in good shape, with three-minute rounds and two-minute breaks in between. In real life, when the first match is over, there may very well be several more immediately following. You don't always have the luxury of going to your corner to rest up or of coming back in another week to find out what to do in part two."

The point of this and other drills conducted under extreme circumstances is to create automatic procedures, for which you have been wired since conception.

Nally's program trains under extreme conditions to help bypass the urge to think and instead leap right into making and executing fast and accurate procedures. And, as all sciences and holistic arts maintain, such procedures will, with repetition, begin triggering in milliseconds—the kind of brain-power you want on your side when entering the world of split-second responses.

Nally's students also use *visualization* in combination with meditation to help them create high-speed procedures. He credits his Judo instructor from years ago for the technique: "If you want to think faster, go home and visualize what you want to happen on the mats," his instructor told him. "See yourself doing it. Then, when opportunity presents itself in real life, you will be able to do it automatically, without thinking."

Nally shares a personal maxim with his students to help them focus their visualizations. I refer to it as The Warrior's Anthem: "Do the right thing, for the right reason, in the right way, with the brilliance of basics, even under extreme conditions."

Visualizations are powerful medicine. You can use your mind like a camera, photographing the object of your attention from every angle. You can see an action from your perspective or from another person's perspective. Using multiple perspectives helps refine techniques. What's more, visualizations can be applied to any situation, on the mats or off.

Visualization works. Recently a Harvard Medical School study showed how a group of individuals doing nothing more than visualizing themselves playing a piano melody improved their ability to perform it as well as another group that practiced it daily. This brings us back to the Skinner box and our uniquely human ability to create fictions and choose what we want to happen from them. The objective is the same: Visualize what you want to happen, and when the opportunity arises, your action will be automatic, freeing up thinking space for other things.

As with biofeedback, Nally teaches how to flow from low energy to high-energy states of attention (theta, beta, and alpha modes)—remember biofeedback's use of machines?—only the colonel's method is a color-coded visualization. Students train using various color codes to help them learn how to flow from one mode of attention to another, with better executive control to ward off premature urges to respond to incoming data.

If you would like to try this visualization, here is how it works:

> **White.** *White is for inattentive. Visualize yourself standing in the center of a white circle, completely detached and drenched in white light, not thinking, and not paying attention to anything—relaxed, as you might feel when you're just staring at your breakfast in the morning for a few slow minutes before you actually remember you are there to eat and get going with your day.*
>
> **Yellow.** *Yellow is for full attention. Visualize yourself standing in the center of a yellow circle, drenched in bright yellow light, with a fully opened field of attention, fully alert, clearheaded, energized, and ready for anything—the way you might feel after a good night's sleep, good breakfast, and your first cup of coffee. This zone is where you want to be most of the time—calm, steady, and ready. When you identify a target (something that needs to be done), you step (not rush or slip) into the next zone, which is orange.*
>
> **Orange.** *Orange is for tightened focus. Visualize yourself stepping into the center of an orange circle. Take a deep breath and charge yourself with energy. Having already zeroed in on something that requires a response, your job now is to scan your entire environment and yourself, choosing the right action, for the right reason. Think basics. Think beyond yourself to others affected by your actions. Choose.*
>
> **Red.** *Red is for execute. Visualize yourself stepping into the center of a red circle. Now, fully alert, fully charged, and decisive, your job is to execute your chosen action and quickly step back into the yellow zone (seeing past the finish line), ready for any backlash and whatever else comes next.*

Black. *Black is for danger. Visualize yourself in the center of a black circle, out of control, mind-blind, either driven into action by destructive emotions like fear, anger, or jealousy, or paralyzed like a deer in headlights. If you feel you have entered this zone, your job is to get out immediately, and return to yellow.*

The idea is to use these color codes to help identify what shifts of attention are available, how to appropriately enter, use, and leave each, and how to commit the sequence to memory. Moreover, you can also use these visuals to identify and adjust your mindset at any given moment. Remember that the more you repeat such drills, the easier and quicker you will be able to toggle between modes—and eventually stop thinking and just pay attention.

One day, not long after I'd interviewed Colonel Nally, I found myself in a father/daughter conversation with Isabella. I was describing for her how much I enjoyed the closeness she, her mother, sister, and I had established as a family. Toward the end of our conversation, she asked me to look at a drawing she had made. But I had just begun to leave the room to head out for work. In one of Dr. Miranda's virtual milliseconds, however, my mind shifted gears. The whole experience was small and very simple, but nonetheless pointed to a new way of responding. Colonel Nally's training program flashed through my mind at warp speed: words and phrases like *teamwork, empathy, see past the finish line and into your next action,* and *do the right thing, in the right way, and for the right reason.*

I put my attention on what I had just told my daughter about family. I considered what I wanted Isabella to take from our conversation. Then, I put my attention on my "self," on what I really wanted most at that moment—an intimate rapport with my daughter and a supportive family. I used my executive attention skills to suppress any immediate urges to leave the room and instead rallied its energy to support a sense of excitement for my daughter's drawing. I felt more in charge of a bigger picture—a greater goal—conducting the moment as Dr. Miranda had said a concert master directs an orchestra. I felt my daughter's confidence as she handed me the drawing and my own confidence in the moment we were creating together. We had bonded. It was what I wanted, what she wanted, and worth every second. Even though there weren't any truly extraordinary circumstances, the moment we had created was. I took a moment and sent the colonel a mental salute.

Putting It All Together

The first step in entering the world of high-speed, accurate perception is to see attention as it is, a fetching system that everyone is born with, collecting data from a river of information flowing through your brain at the tune of 11 million bits per second. But attention is not an exotic gift. It is an essential part of what it means to be human. It is a skill that enables you and me to take in the world as well as allows the world to penetrate us. Consequently, like all skills, your power of attention develops incrementally, and you can choose to develop it or not.

Good attention is controlled attention that is guided by good choices.

By consciously guiding selective data into your mind, you can play a significant role in how successful your day-to-day experiences will be. This kind of attention-management fosters high self-esteem, confidence, better working procedures, faster thinking, and a positive world view. It puts you much more in charge of your own destinies—big and small. What's more, each of these benefits naturally compounds.

On the flip side, when you choose to be inattentive, you essentially give away your power to choose immediate actions, reactions, and even the procedures that will be stored for future high-speed use. In short, you hand the steering wheel of your life over to someone or something else, significantly cutting off how you really feel and what you really need. And, of course, this lack of control generates lower self-esteem, lower confidence, less effective (or ineffective) working procedures, and, as a result, slower thinking, and a downbeat view of the world. These negative effects will also naturally compound. Consider the toll of 30 or 40 years of this kind of living.

Although there is no magic potion that zaps your attention control into overnight perfection, this book contends that knowing even a little about how your system of attention works enables you to make it run strikingly better.

Peering into the attentive brain, there is no single switch you can flip on or off that will regulate every component of your attentional mechanism. Instead, you will discover a series of links you can gate to maximize your attention per situation. To this end, reflection is key. Through reflection, you can scan the sensory data you have pumped into your field of attention. You can see how you have gated this data, as well as check what links in the chain are pulling their weight and which are not. This gives you the opportunity to make adjustments, as well as to suppress and block when necessary. Reflection allows you to keep, edit, or compose new high-speed procedures to help you achieve forthcoming goals.

With this in mind, both ancient arts and cutting-edge science identify meditation as one of the best nonmedical ways to achieve reflection and carry over its benefits into daily life. Research shows attention meditation can be used to tap into and change brainwave patterns (from high-alert patterns to ultra-relaxed) upon command in the very same way that biofeedback can. What's more, practice can make your ability to shift from high to low modes an automatic part of your daily routines.

Other tools, besides meditation, that enable you to maximize your field of attention are: mushin, measured breathing, and visualization.

Both arts and sciences insist that self-awareness is the hub of all attention tools and links. This is because self-awareness leads to empathy, which opens your field to include the feelings of others. Together your self-awareness and empathy tell you what information in your environments (internal and external) is relevant, what isn't, and what procedures to generate as a result. This, of course, brings us back to that early morning in my kitchen and Isabella's tantalizing reminder of the mindset from which we have all come and to which martial arts and cutting-edge sciences can help us return.

To be sure, high-speed, sharp thinking is an outgrowth of executive attention and good training. But what happens when attention skills go wrong? And more importantly, how do we get them back on track? Let's take a look.

YOUR HORMONES
DON'T SPEAK ENGLISH

If the mind depends on the brain, then all aspects
of the mind are going to depend on these simple
electrical, chemical processes.
—Joseph LeDoux

See With Your Skin

Consider this: There are two black belts squared off on the mats. Evenly ranked, their martial arts skills are virtually equal. One is female and the other male. The female throws a towering kick at her opponent. He attempts to block it, and she immediately kicks low with her other leg, sweeping his feet from under him. He lands on his back, staring up at the ceiling, wondering what just happened. He rises very pumped up and aggressive, wanting to fire back. Her brain orders a stream of hormones to help keep it lit and focused. She feels the urge to attack but the chemicals now cascading through her blood keep her cool and attentive. Brain circuits capable of blurring her body movements with her opponent's turn on so that to her mind's eye she and her opponent meld into one image. This allows her access to what he has in mind. Even though it is still a split-second before he does anything, she already knows he is going to attack, where the attack will come from (right, left, high, low), and what motor skills she will need to evade him in order to take him out once and for all. He, on the other hand, has blocked or inhibited a river of information that he might find useful in putting him on equal footing. Without thinking, he attacks. Her blood chemistry changes again— this time to facilitate her retreat and counter moves. She arches back and sidesteps him. Out of harm's way before he even finishes his attack, she launches a high-speed procedure that results in several strikes to her opponent and a big judo-throw take-down finale.

To a bystander, she seems like the superior player, and for this match-up she certainly has been. But the two players are hardwired to the same capacity. Their martial arts skill is virtually equal. One possible explanation for her dominance in this match, however, is that she has used her attention to listen more closely to her brain's signaling circuits, and he has not. Her reward: victory. But the story doesn't stop there.

Her blood chemistry changes yet again and her mood shifts— she is high on the win. This is because her brain's reward mechanism has streamed a feel-good elixir into her nerve cells and left it there for a while—creating an upbeat, hormonal tidal wave. Endocrine research shows that this reward will motivate her to follow similar procedures again, which will potentially gather further successes on the mats, more rewards, more motivation, and build greater confidence in the future.

But how do you listen to these brain circuits and what are they saying? And how can this body-talk lead to better thinking, better decision-making, and ultimately to more successful actions and happier living?

Such "listening" requires you to orient your attention from what's going on outside of you to what's going on inside. Psychologists refer to this movement as *toggling from exogenous* (data outside the body, brain) *to endogenous* (inside). Martial artists simply call it *sensitivity*, and sensitivity training is essential to all martial arts. My sensei's idea of sensitivity began with what he referred to as "seeing with your skin."

"You need more sensitivity. Eyes are deceptive. See with your skin," he would say over and over until it sank into your reflexes.

The word *sensitivity* itself can be traced to the Latin *sens*, meaning "to feel." It is, perhaps, best understood as ultra-close listening to what you are feeling internally as well as to everything happening externally.

In many ways, sensitivity is a language unto itself. I remember when my instructor first introduced the concept.

"Focus on your feet," he said. "What do you feel beneath them?"

"The floor," I answered.

He asked me to close my eyes.

"Now what can you feel?"

After a few moments of silence, I added, "I can feel the bottoms of my feet, the air surrounding them, and the blood flowing through them."

"That's good. Now make yourself feel more," he said. "What else can you feel?"

"My skin and muscle," I said.

"What more?"

"My legs, hips, weight, the rest of my body—torso, shoulders, arms, hands, head, my breath, you—I have some sense of you," I added. "And the building and the various machines in the building, the energy below it and above it, the breeze coming in through the window."

"That's it," he said.

Seeing with your skin means to use more than just your eyes to observe and listen to others. You can sense with deeper attention. Use all of you. The more you can focus on what you feel, the better you will be at determining your actions or if you need to act at all. Sensitivity quickens your mind and develops a more accurate intuition.

Once, my sensei asked me to stand a few inches away from him. He closed his eyes and placed a hand on my chest, instructing me strike at him. I threw a high punch, and he met it with an immediate block.

"Throw any kind of strike you want," he said.

It didn't matter if I kicked, punched, or reached to grab, he was able to predict all my moves before I did anything.

"Once you make contact with an opponent, you should be able to sense what his or her next action will be," he insisted.

At first, I thought we trained sensitivity simply to improve martial speed and accuracy. Although that was part of it, little did I know that the exercises were ultimately designed to help us train our brains for use beyond the mats.

What Makes You Lose Attention

Science has shown and continues to show that many of our decisions and behaviors are influenced by cognitive, chemical, emotional, and motivational processes that steep alongside our field awareness. Putting your focus on these underlying mechanisms is an important part of attention training.

Consider this scenario: You are quietly driving down the highway. Perhaps you are thinking about a slow, relaxing dinner you will have when you arrive home. Maybe you are not thinking at all. Your car windows are down. There is a lovely breeze. The sky is bright with a few billowing clouds, the kind that when you were a child looked like cotton candy. Suddenly, out of nowhere, a siren begins screaming behind you. You check the review mirror and spot a state police car with flashing lights quickly approaching. Heavy traffic surrounds you. You feel an overwhelming sense of urgency. For a moment, you don't know which way to turn. Inside your body, an alert system goes off. Adrenal glands begin streaming cortisol (a steroid hormone) to your brain to spring you into action. Then your body launches an immediate tranquilizing hormone to help suppress your adrenal glands before your cortisol levels get too pushy and send you into a paralyzing overdrive. The state police car is now right behind you, and, trying to veer out of its path, you almost cause an accident. You feel as though you are being hit with a tidal wave of stress. You feel anything but like yourself.

Other hormones begin rushing to your brain to round up the remnants of cortisol that made it to your hippocampus. These hormones guide the cortisol back to your kidneys where they resided before they were called into action. Their job is to keep you from hitting overdrive and bring you back to a place of balance that scientists call *homeostasis*. But this isn't always an easy task. Before equilibrium is achieved, your brain attempts to tag on to either the stimulating or tranquilizing chemical force. This results in an imbalance in which one of these forces will dominate the other for a while without relief. The discontinuity furthers your stress and can have serious consequences on your attention for as long as it lasts.

Why can't you just snap back into balance? There are two reasons upon which your mind depends. One is electrical and the other is chemical, and they comprise two distinct brain functions—both of which provide you with data. They are also located in two different parts of the brain and are not always in synch.

You may have heard of these components referred to as the reasoning part of your brain, what scientists call the *neocortex* (specializing in language skills), and the emotional part of your brain, or the *limbic* (specializing in feelings). A disconnect occurs because your brain doesn't know which message to pay attention to. Your neocortex may be firing one signal, "Whew, that was a close one, but at least it's over," while the limbic system, which is much slower, is sending another. And so at times like this, the big question is: Who do you listen to?

Consider this variation of Dr. Miranda's earlier comparison: Imagine listening to a symphony, with a 100-piece orchestra. Much of the time you are just taking in the whole wave of music coming at you. But you know that at any given moment you could, at will, put your attention on just the violins or just the percussion or any single component of the ensemble. Then you could reassemble the whole wave of sound and with fuller appreciation of the role violins (or any chosen instrument) have in creating the total unified effect. This is to say that you would better understand the interaction among instruments you never gave much attention to before. Remember, you are the director.

You don't need a million-dollar imaging machine to understand what's going on in your head. You just have to train your attention to be a little more sensitive to what's activating in your brain and the rest of your body during certain moments. This will help you see how much teamwork is going on in your head and how you can begin to self-regulate these processes to your greatest advantage.

Your Hormones Don't Speak English

Remember that famous commercial: "This is your brain. This is your brain on drugs"? Although the commercial made its point, a worthy one, for many Americans, there was a certain irony about it. The fact was that neuroscience has proven without doubt that your brain is naturally always on drugs. In a way, this sounds funny, especially in the aftermath of all the anti-drug sentiment commercialized during the Reagan years. Yet MIT professor Marvin Minsky, a philosopher and one of the most important researchers in the area of computer science, believes that human beings are all just basically a "mass of chemicals and switches."[1] And as far as the scientific world is concerned he is in good company. In a recent *New York Times* interview, all-star neurologist Dr. Joseph LeDoux, professor of neuroscience at NYU, echoed Minsky's belief—with a bit of humor. LeDoux's father was a butcher, and as a youth LeDoux worked for him, cleaning off cow brains. And so it was interesting, almost ironic, to see his comment: "That's what the brain is," he said, "just a piece of meat that has chemicals and electric charges."[2] The history of this view of the brain, to which both Minsky and LeDoux refer, is somewhat interesting in and of itself. Research into the brain's capacity to self-produce what are now known as pleasure drugs was prompted in the early 1970s—this by government concern over the numbers of Vietnam veterans returning home addicted to opiates such as heroine and morphine. At the time, scientists knew little about how and why opiates worked and particularly about how they affect the brain.

What they did know was that opium came from poppy seeds and that it could be made into a powder and put into into pills, or it could be made into a serum. Opiates like morphine and heroin have generally been used medically, as well as recreationally, to produce a feeling of euphoria and to relieve pain.

Again in the 1970s, with the discovery of endorphins (morphine produced by the body), scientists got a first glance into the brain's ability to produce its own highs. Not only that, but in subsequent years, further research would turn up at least 20 other such locks—indicating that the brain's capacity to generate its own pharmaceuticals extends beyond just opium derivatives.

Popular interest in the body's ability to create "natural highs" circulated widely and continues unto this day—more so, perhaps, than any other single detail of brain science.

One of the most widely publicized effects of natural highs is the so-called runner's high, said to kick in when strenuous exercise takes you over the top of what you're used to and activates endorphin production. This happens when your level of exercise is between moderate to high and muscles have used up stored glycogen (a carbohydrate that quickly converts to sugar). Not limited to just running, the sensation can be generated by any intense physical activity such as aerobics, sparring, wrestling, football, weight lifting, swimming, bicycling, gymnastics, basketball, and so on. Bottom line: If a person wants the effects of endorphins he or she can make them at will. Another point worth noting is that if you meet someone high on endorphins, he or she is under the influence of powerful chemistry. Using PET scans combined with recently available chemicals, a 2008 study conducted in Germany concluded that runner's high is real and yields deep pleasure.[3]

Several studies have been conducted to see if runner's high might produce a brain chemical similar to THC, the active chemical found in marijuana. However, findings have been mixed. You may be amused to know some studies report such a chemical has in fact been found in chocolate.

In the 1960s and 1970s a lot of drug slang started appearing everywhere in the language. Terms such *junkie, laced, mind-numbing, blown away, spiked, mind-blowing*—and the list goes on—had found a place in popular dialect. Today, you can see just how much clout endocrine jargon carries in our daily appraisals of things when terms like *adrenaline rush, estrogen*, and *testosterone* have dropped into everyday language—sometimes not necessarily in the most pleasant of ways. Probably every office in the country has, at one time or another, heard its version of sexist neuro-bantering: "If you're smart you'll stay away from her; she must be pregnant—again," or "it's the PMS talking," or "his testosterone is flying," or the even more vulgar "he's talking with his head between his legs." The body's top-shelf, self-producing pleasure drugs have become more familiar in ordinary chit-chat as well. Terms such as *serotonin, cortisol, oxytocin*, and *dopamine*, which will appear in the coming pages, lead the lineup.

It is good to remember that the brain is, of course, better at regulating the drugs it produces than individuals who have decided to pursue the use of drugs recreationally. It is clear from stats citing the long-term and irreversible psycho-biological damage and even deaths inflicted by drug overdose each year that recreational drug abuse poses serious problems and must be discouraged. However, in an ironic twist, of which Steven Johnson wittily writes in his book, *Mind Wide Open*, "We should not be so quick to imagine the rhetoric of drug use as some alien, unnatural experience, far outside the boundaries of the 'straight' world. Beneath all the drug war rhetoric, there is this sobering—or is it intoxicating?—thought: If you could [scan] your brain at the happiest moments of your life, the images would probably look remarkably similar to brain scans of people doing heroin or cocaine for the first time."[4]

Johnson's point is well taken and can be applied to anyone trying to sharpen his or her attentional skills. Indeed, cutting-edge research insists that the brain's naturally produced chemicals explain a wide variety of our behaviors—both functional and dysfunctional. Picture this: As you sit pondering the ideas of this book, your own brain is awash in a stream of various chemicals—any of which is powerful enough to require a license to prescribe.

Endocrine research shows that when the body produces too much or too little of these chemicals, attentional problems are likely to occur. So again, part of paying attention is being able to focus on and listen to what drugs the brain is being influenced by at any particular moment, and especially during times of important motivation and decision-making. Prompts may come in the form of a chemical or a mood shift, or shades of both. Whichever way they come, the first step is to recognize them and see how they correspond to your thoughts, feelings, and actions.

The Adrenaline Rush

Adrenaline is what's referred to as your *fight-or-flight* hormone. Its job is to increase breathing, heart rate, and blood pressure, and move more oxygen-rich blood to the brain and to the muscles when needed. To give you more overall "oomph," adrenaline generates the release of glucose and fatty acid into your bloodstream. Bear in mind that an appropriate adrenaline rush is a healthy and necessary part of life.

In the world of sports, for example, the adrenaline rush is nothing new. Athletes learn early on that getting pumped up has many advantages. A martial artist, for instance, learns that when adrenaline is flowing, you can punch harder and faster, increase your flexibility, better read your opponent, and better orchestrate your next move. High on adrenaline, sensory information is keener, memory is sharper, and you are less sensitive to pain—all good for sporting as well as other life interests. Performers of all types (musicians, dancers, writers, public speakers, and the like) know that getting your adrenaline flowing can lead to successful results.

But there is another side to adrenaline, and most of us are familiar with that side as well. Too much adrenaline, feeling too pumped, so to speak, can contaminate your capacity to attend, weakening your ability to match your best procedures with pressing goals. Soaring on adrenaline can leave you prone to things that are not in your best interest: A weightlifter, for example, may think he can lift more than he is capable; a runner may break into a final sprint earlier than what may be strategically appropriate to win the race; a CEO may optimistically seal a deal before all her vital data is in. A lesser-known fact is that once you are high on adrenaline, you tend to groove experiences deeper into your memory; potentially making certain experiences last for life. In terms of recall, when you are high on adrenaline such memories bubble up even more quickly and also more intensely. So adrenaline can be tricky. Research shows that a certain amount of the hormone is, however, necessary to reach one's maximum physical and mental performance. You experience this when going into a test feeling a bit anxious and then, seeing that the first couple of questions are manageable, you calm down. The next thing you know, you are feeling the effects of just the right amount of adrenaline and are sailing—unless you hit a question that throws you off again. So again, it's a little tricky. Too much adrenaline can interfere with your ability to attend and potentially impede your performance.

Your adrenal glands will turn on whenever you perceive a situation as stressful. This is your fight-or-flight apparatus kicking in. If stressors persist after a few minutes, however, your adrenals may stream another chemical into your blood to remedy the problem: cortisol.

The Stress Hormone

Have you ever forgotten a piece of important information in mid-sentence? Too much cortisol in your bloodstream could be the reason.

Cortisol is often referred to as the "stress hormone," as it is involved in your body's healthy response to stress. And similar to adrenaline, a certain amount of cortisol is necessary for peak performance. This is because cortisol helps strengthen memory as well as spike and maintain alertness. On the other hand, a mountain of evidence shows that over-secretion of cortisol has been linked to a wide range of physical and mental damage caused by long-term anxiety.

MRC Health Services Research Collaboration at the University of Bristol has conducted extensive research in the affects of cortisol production on attention. Data shows, according to Dr. K. Vedhara and fellow researchers at MRC, that working memory, as well as selective and divided attentional processes, are indeed impaired by lower levels of cortisol. But again, too much cortisol production isn't better.[5] Dr. Robert Sapolsky, professor of neurology and neurological sciences at Stanford University, has shown that sustained stress can interfere with learning and memory.[6] Acting to decrease the processing of significant information, too much cortisol can interfere with your brain cells' ability to communicate with each other. This sort of thing can happen in the middle of a lecture, presentation, or in everyday conversation—such as when you are in the middle of describing a three-step process or three important things to remember and then suddenly can only remember two. A common sort of blip in attention, when such things occur they can be associated with excessive cortisol production.

Too much cortisol can also impair the retrieval of long-term memories as well as set off your fight-or-flight's freeze alarm. The end result is anger-like feelings (fight), fear-like feelings (flight), and the inability to do anything about it. This happens when a person is paralyzed in his or her anger or fears—as in the account of a person fleeing a tiger. What's more, it may only take a millisecond for you to choke up.

Cortisol streams blood glucose to the muscles; hence, energy that would reach the hippocampus is lessened. This is good, say, if you are about to do something athletic. On the other hand, too much cortisol can compromise your hippocampus's ability to create new memories as well as decrease your working memory—usually the first kind of memory loss associated with aging, as well as stress. McGill psychiatry professor Sonia Lupien explains: "Long-term exposure to these hormones can cause atrophy of the hippocampus, leading to memory impairment."[7] In addition, Lupien reports that hippocampal damage is one of the early signs of Alzheimer's. Interesting and worthy of most peoples' concern, the interchange between stress and cortisol tracks like a perfect storm—or perhaps more like a perfect tsunami. Here's why: The brain's hypothalamus usually responds to stress by causing the pituitary gland to send another chemical telling the adrenals to secrete cortisol. If these levels start to get too high, several areas of the brain, especially the hippocampus, tell the hypothalamus to turn off the cortisol-producing mechanism. This is the proper response. However, research indicates that a constant exposure to cortisol can damage brain cells to the extent that these functions can no longer provide proper feedback to control cortisol production, and this can send a person into a downward spin, causing more damage to the hippocampus, causing more unwanted cortisol, and beginning a degenerative storm that can, in the end, be very difficult to stop or regulate. One common key ingredient in memory loss has been low self-esteem. To this end, researchers have discovered that supportive social environments have been able to make a difference. Like adrenaline, cortisol is attentionally functional, yet should be monitored when possible. Too much, however, can defocus you and even result in more serious attentional problems. The right amount of cortisol, however, can boost arousal and actually help you attend to stress.

Listening to Serotonin

Ever feel scatterbrained, poorly organized, and unfocused? This may be due to low levels of serotonin.

Serotonin came into everyday talk largely through its association with Prozac, which works by increasing the amount of serotonin available to the brain. In his book *Change Your Brain, Change Your Life*, Dr. Daniel G. Amen notes that "Low levels of serotonin are often associated with worrying, moodiness, emotional rigidity, and irritability (a combination of deep limbic and cingulate problems)."[8] This means that when serotonin is low it interferes with your abilities to reason and respond to things emotionally. Specifically, low levels of the drug can impair your ability to effectively use your attention to help in matters of decision-making, empathy, anticipation of reward, and emotional responses.

According to researchers, the effects of serotonin are often quite strong, making its presence easier to detect. And this is a plus for those of us trying to be more attentive to the effect of this hormone in our day-to-day lives.

In Peter Kramer's famous book, *Listening to Prozac*, Kramer urges people to "listen" to the effects of such hormones.[9] The point is that by listening, Kramer believes Prozac patients can do better than just alleviate problems such as depression. Listening helps with the bigger picture, and that is the struggle to understand self. And so when he insists that listening to your body chemistry will produce a better understanding of self, Kramer speaks to all of us. The point is that by recognizing which of your specific (selective) behaviors (procedures) generate problems—attentional, social, or otherwise—and which behaviors you may have been born with, you can treat the source of behaviors you want to take control of rather than just their symptoms.

Rejection-sensitive people find their reactions to disappointing news or personal slights fade under the influence of Prozac—that is, with higher levels of serotonin. They become less sensitive and more confident, as well as more inclined to take risks, but not recklessly or without perspective.

Drugs such as Prozac make certain behavioral patterns stand out. Thus, by listening to your body chemistry, you can not only see the problem but alleviate it as well. In a way, you can wind up better than before because you now understand how your personal body chemistry affects your behavior. By putting your attention on the affects of these chemicals that are an integral part of you, you have a better chance of identifying root causes behind daily thoughts, feelings, and actions you may like to modify or even eliminate.

It occurs to me that, in a way, this process of listening could be likened to a chemical version of biofeedback: Once you learn to put your attention on how you feel before and after your brain self-medicates, as well as the effects of each of its naturally produced chemicals, you can begin to take better control of your responses, in terms of thoughts, feelings, and actions. It's like once you have isolated a violin in a symphony—you don't have to guide your attention to it anymore. You just hear it.

According to Dr. Stanley Glick, director of the Center for Neuropharmacology and Neuroscience at Albany Medical College, serotonin facilitates attention because "it helps awaken and maintain arousal. It can facilitate selective attention by helping you see something as relevant or irrelevant. LSD, for example, disrupts this mechanism."[10]

Conversely, low levels of serotonin can foster aggressive behavior. And high doses have been found to heighten sensitivity and overreacting.

In the world of brain science, Glick is high-torque, bringing decades of research, a PhD, and an MD to the table. Soft-spoken and congenial, he has a gift of being able to make some pretty tough science palatable to laypeople. In an October 2007 article about his work at AMC, he asserts that "There's evidence that drugs of abuse take over pathways in the brain that normally give us pleasure."

To this end, he has conducted years of research to prove that addiction is a metabolic disease of the brain, and he has worked to develop new drugs to treat addiction, as well as understand why certain people are more prone to addiction than others.

I questioned Glick about this. "I don't drink much alcohol," I said. "However, if I were debating whether or not to drink a few beers, let's say, before driving my car, I would go through a whole grocery list of logic, and, in the end, conclude that I just can't do a thing like that."

"That's what distinguishes you from an addict," Glick insists. "You can 'just say no,' but an addict's neurochemistry won't let him just say no."

This brings us back to the idea of being able to selectively put your attention on incoming data and choose what you want to happen next—what Dr. Tram Neill referred to as the feeling of being in control.

Glick throws up a caution, however, saying that the brain's complicated circuitry makes balance hard to achieve.

"If I were going to drive under the influence of anything— let's use alcohol as an example—could I, knowing how alcohol will impair me, regulate my actions, let's say better than if I had never had a sip of alcohol before in my life? It seems to me that part of feeling in control would involve knowing what to expect next."

Glick pointed out that research shows what you experience is what you expect.

In one popular test, for example, on the effects of adrenaline, adrenaline was administered to one group of individuals, and a placebo (sugar pill) to another group. Afterward, the group given nothing more than a placebo reported experiencing adrenaline effects.

Similar testing has been done on the effects of marijuana. For example, a well-known test used two groups of individuals. One group was given lettuce leaves and told it was marijuana, and the other was given actual marijuana. Results were similar to the adrenaline test; that is, the group given only lettuce reported experiencing a marijuana high.

Science refers to our ability to compensate for things that we expect to happen as behavioral tolerance, and it turns out that compensation is part of listening to your body chemistry.

To explain this part of the picture, Glick drew on an experiment in which 100 drivers were given a dose of marijuana and then put through a driver test. The way things worked out, one third of the group experienced impaired driving, another third experienced no effect on their driving, and another third drove better. The group whose driving was impaired didn't quite know what to expect in terms of the drug's effects. The other two groups, however, did, and were able to compensate for what they expected to happen—thus, they drove more slowly, more cautiously, more attentively, and so on.

By listening to your body's chemistry, you can bring into your field of attention patterns of physiology that signal specific thoughts, feelings, and actions. Just knowing, for example, that the release of a particular hormone into my bloodstream may last up to 10 minutes tells me that I will be "under the influence," so to speak, for a certain period of time, and helps me gauge what to expect next. Putting my attention on this information, in turn, helps me better select actions that are in my best interests. But what do I listen for?

According to Glick, I am more likely to feel peripheral responses to the release of hormones. With adrenaline, I may feel cardiovascular effects such as an increase in heart rate, blood pressure, ventilation, stress, and so on. If after a rewarding situation, I feel euphoric, it's likely that dopamine has been released.

Everyday life is full of examples. If every time you go into a conference meeting you begin to feel a cascade of hormones making you aggressive and argumentative, putting your attention on this behavioral pattern and thinking about how to compensate for it prior to your next meeting might help you orchestrate more successful actions in the future. Keep in mind: Serotonin can help maintain arousal, too little serotonin can foster aggression, and high doses have been found to heighten sensitivity and overreacting.

Euphoria

Picture this: You have been waiting for a promotion for several years. Finally the day arrives and you receive it. The feeling is delicious. And you are high about your accomplishment. This "high" is partly due to the release of another self-produced brain drug, dopamine, into your bloodstream.

Dopamine causes extreme pleasure and is associated with reward-seeking behaviors that, according to researchers, may help explain the biological mechanism behind the way the brain uses rewards in decision-making. Like a pleasure-coach keeping score of every "game" you enter, dopamine helps drive you to get what you want, and not to avoid what you fear. When you get what you want, a surge of dopamine rewards you, and the feeling is euphoric. Anticipation, however, can make your brain's production of the hormone somewhat fickle. For example, if you achieve less than what you expect out of an experience, your dopamine levels drop accordingly. If you achieve more than you anticipate—get a bigger promotion, higher grade, better product, and such—your brain produces extra.

Scientists now know dopamine can play a major role in how you attend to things. It can orchestrate what you see as most important internally or externally. It can influence your thoughts, how you participate in events, and what information you see as relevant or irrelevant. Even your dreams can be brushed with dopamine. South African neurologist Mark Sloms reports that the brain has developed a seeking system, "an orchestration of primitive and higher neural structures that orient us to the outside world with an air of anticipation and positive expectancy. It's an all-purpose looking-for-pleasure-in-this-world drive...."[11] And therein attentional problems can occur. If, for example, you expect a perfect-10 day and instead are hit with a perfect dud accompanied by a parking ticket at the end of your day, you may feel the doldrums of lower dopamine levels. Of further consequence, your attention can be goaded into looking for reward wherever it can get it. It seems that just knowing this can change your outlook as well as reactions on days when you expect a lot and come up short.

Research shows low levels of the hormone are also associated with depression, lack of motivation, and trouble focusing. Personally speaking, the effects of this brain tendency come to mind often now when I am dealing with situations that fall below my expectations. And just that little reminder has helped keep me more motivated and positive when attending to things on these sorts of days—and prevented me from chasing after sometimes pretty extraneous rewards.

Ohio-based psychologist Dr. Joseph M. Carver reports that low levels of dopamine impair your ability to attend to tasks, activities, and even conversation, making focus and concentration difficult.[12] Additionally, Sharon Begley writes in her book, *Train Your Mind, Change Your Brain*, "When dopamine circuits go awry, addiction can result: an addict's dopamine circuits become so inured to the pleasures of alcohol, shopping, or opiates, that he requires more and more [dopamine] or activity to get the same kick."[13] The joyless worldview of many older adults may be in part due to what Begley refers to as a "sluggish dopamine system."

High levels of dopamine are associated with delusional (inflated) behavior and thinking. Carver insists that when levels begin to rise, we become "excited, energized, then suspicious and paranoid, and then hyper-stimulated by our environment." Whereas low levels make it hard to focus, high levels make our focus so intense and tight (narrow) that we don't know what is important from what is not.[14]

Listening to the peripheral effects of dopamine can help you better deal with issues of excitement or joylessness and generate better motivation, mental clarity, and conflict resolution. Additionally, you can better understand and manage thrill-seeking behaviors, especially if and when they lead to all the wrong places.

Me Venus, You Mars?

Mounds of scientific research report that effects of the sex hormones estrogen, testosterone, and oxytocin extend beyond reproduction and can also affect the brain's attentional system. What's more, effects are somewhat predictable, and this makes listening to this set of hormones even easier. But does that mean that men and women are from different neurochemical planets? Let's take a look.

Estrogen is the sex hormone commonly associated with females. Principally produced by the ovaries, it is responsible for stimulating the growth of female sex organs, breasts, and regulating menstruation as well as a female's secondary sex characteristics. What some people don't know about estrogen is that it is also produced in men by their adrenal glands and testicles. However, because it appears in much smaller amounts in men and apparently has no function—except for in extremely high levels where it has been connected to loss of sexual appetite—it is not of major concern.

For women, though, estrogen has long been associated with the ability to handle stress and keep memory sharp. Dr. Sally Shaywitz, professor of pediatrics at the Yale School of Medicine, reports that when estrogen is at its highest—just before ovulation—there is an increase in verbal fluency, speed of communication, and working memory.[15]

The sex hormone mostly associated with men is testosterone. It is produced in the testes and is responsible for the development of the male sex organs as well as secondary gender characteristics such as depth of voice and facial hair. Surprisingly the hormone is also secreted from the adrenal glands in women, only in much smaller amounts.

One of the most well-known characteristics of testosterone is its link to dominance and aggressive behavior. Its effects, however, can be shaded. For example, research recognizes that testosterone ramps up aggression in status-seeking men. But tests conducted by Dr. Robert Josephs and partners of the psychology department at the University of Texas, Austin, show this is so when participants— men *and* women—high on testosterone, perceived themselves in high-status tasks.[16] It's all in the perception. When they saw themselves in a lower-status activity, they were distracted, less able to concentrate, and performance declined. Individuals with lower levels of testosterone don't seem to be affected this way. When I asked Josephs about this, he was clear: Only people high on testosterone performed negatively in positions where they saw themselves as followers and their high-status persona in jeopardy. Interestingly, low-testosterone individuals, Josephs explained, experienced the same strong reactions when placed in high-status positions. Research shows that testosterone levels drop in those who don't care whether they win or lose, but spike in those who want to dominate. This last detail fascinates me because it is one of the first big lessons you learn after you have mastered the basics in martial arts training. Up to this point you have been mostly concerned with externals, technique, other people, and environment. Now, in the next phase, you begin to listen to your internal workings. Here the big lesson is detachment; you learn to detach from the idea of winning or losing. In fact, to emphasize the point, my sensei used to say there is no such thing as winning or losing—just participating.

Josephs is sharp and witty and able to make explorations into endocrinology quite entertaining. He strikes me as the type of teacher that students would enjoy working with. He really hit the target for me when he semi-humorously told me a story about how one of the things that attracted him to the study of psychology in the first place was the capacity of a person to be so affected by his or her biochemistry that in a matter of moments that person could begin acting like someone else entirely. Then, that person could snap right back to his or her usual modus operandi without ever realizing any of it. I had certainly encountered a few "Jeckle and Hyde" moments in my life experience—most of us probably have. A friend of mine chuckled when I relayed the story to him, and then told me that he has been working with someone like that for five years. Whenever a superior reprimands the guy, my friend explained, "he goes on a hyper-fit that last days and is often afterward clouded by weak judgment." For example, "We could finish a project under budget, save the company all kinds of monies, and be reprimanded for not having had the budget accurate. We could finish a project on budget and be reprimanded for not being able to save. Things like that. After a few days, when he is back to normal, he's completely unaware of why people are keeping their distance." It occurred to me that it's not that much different than if you were to accidentally slip someone who doesn't use caffeine some caffeinated coffee without his knowing. The drug would have its effect, wear off, and he wouldn't be any the wiser—unless he were training himself to listen to his body chemistry regularly.

The drive to dominate, however, Josephs insists, is only realized if you have the courage to approach your goal. And testosterone's effects can be shaded. According to Josephs, high cortisol drives approach-avoidance and can cause you to choke under pressure. Low cortisol will fuel aggressive behavior, says Josephs. The newest research Josephs and University of Texas partners have conducted shows that low testosterone–high cortisol combination levels predicate choking under pressure, whereas high testosterone, low cortisol levels help you pull it together in a low-odds situation.

Bill Clinton is a good example of this. He has given some of his best speeches of his life within 24 hours of some of the worst situations that faced him. Tiger Woods is another example, making some of his best shots under the most pressure without flinching.

Tests conducted at the University of California, San Francisco, show that older men with naturally higher testosterone levels have heightened concentration, memory, and other attentional skills. Higher levels of testosterone were also found to help reduce the risk of cognitive decline and Alzheimer's disease in older men.[17]

However, high testosterone levels seem to have a reverse affect on young men, whereas lower testosterone levels apparently increase their spatial skills. Women, on the other hand, with higher testosterone levels demonstrate enhanced spatial abilities.

As a footnote, research shows that you can increase your testosterone levels naturally with exercise.

Oxytocin, a major hormone secreted by the pituitary gland, may be the most popular of the brain's pleasure drugs. It is released rapidly during sexual climax, child birth, breastfeeding, touch, and massage. Receptors located in the brain's dopamine camp team up and amplify the good feelings these activities bring and can produce a rich sense of calm and nurturing.

For decades it was believed that the fight-or-flight syndrome applied equally to men and women. But in a compelling study appearing in the *Psychological Review* led by Dr. Shelley Taylor, a University of California psychology professor and author of *Tending Instinct*, found differently. Its findings were based on hundreds of responses to stress by thousands of human and animal subjects. What Taylor and her research partners discovered was that women are more likely to deal with stressors by applying "tend and befriend" actions rooted in nurturing and seeking social contact, particularly with other women. Additionally, yes, women, similar to men, also react to stress with a rapid release of adrenaline and cortisol. But then enters oxytocin, which affects women more than men. Taylor reports that in women, estrogen heightens oxytocin's feel-good effects by toning down the release of adrenaline and other stress hormones into the bloodstream and amping up the tend-or-befriend response. In men, however, testosterone seems to diminish oxytocin's effect. As such, women's sex hormones give them an advantage at handling stress, which can translate to better attending to incoming data under the influence of fight-or-flight feelings.[18]

In general, men and women with higher levels of oxytocin are more social as well as more trusting.

Listening to gender-related hormones intelligently will put closer attention on how you feel in a wide variety of environments, and during certain times and seasons. Listening with intelligence will enable you to match priority activities with the best time and place to achieve your best performance.

But do we really live in an endocrine jungle in which men and women are so different that gender will predetermine the way we act and feel about everything? It doesn't seem likely. But there is no doubt that listening to each other's biochemistry can help us learn from each other's differences and begin to appreciate each other more in light of them. This can only enhance our ability as individuals to relate to as well as appreciate and love each other more. Good listening will help you reflect on what to expect and how you can compensate in your attempt to match hormone levels, environments, and goals, as Josephs puts it, to make things more "hormonious."

THE EMOTIONAL FACTOR

Indeed there is now vast and clear research showing that when it comes to making decisions and influencing behaviors, feelings count as much, and maybe even more, than thought.
—Daniel Goleman

The Emotional Factor

We've all felt emotions. Indeed, everyone has experienced love, hate, happiness, disgust, and fear. Such feelings are the strong stuff that can shape many aspects of your mental and physical wellbeing. They can exert their influence on your perception, memory, why you take one action over another, and even your dreams. By looking at the way emotions work in the brain, you can better understand how they affect your attention and guide your focus, at times without your conscious involvement. Such understanding can help you turn your emotions into a great attentional tool and as a result help you maximize your thoughts and actions as you attend to things on a daily basis.

In recent years, scientists have learned a lot about where emotion comes from and why it is necessary. Psychologists turn to evolution for a clue. What they have discovered is that many of our emotional responses are linked to primitive survival mechanisms—fear, for example, pumping more blood through the body; anger racing us into overdrive, making our fight-or-flight behaviors more proficient.

Scientists refer to the area of the brain connected to these responses as the *limbic system*, and its headquarters as the *amygdala*, a part of the forebrain named as such because its shape resembles that of an almond. A very old part of the brain in terms of evolutionary development, the amygdala holds the keys to happiness, sadness, fear, anger, and disgust.

As that part of the brain known as the *cerebral cortex* (commonly referred to as *gray matter*) evolved, we gained the capacity to problem-solve, organize, plan, and remember through rational thought. But one must have motivation, emotion, and desire for these to occur. And it is our limbic system that lights our fire, so to speak, and marks our individual emotional disposition.

Although both areas of the brain work closely together, they have different functions. For example, the emotion of fear grows from your limbic system, but accurately locating the target of your fear—or fearful thoughts you may have about it—involve the cerebral cortex. Lust grows from the limbic system, whereas being able to identify whether you are in love is from the cerebral cortex, which, research indicates, has access to memory as well as reason. But the two systems are not always in synch. And as such they can play tricks on us.

Irrational Fear

One evening this past summer, while mowing the lawn I felt a sudden spiky pain in my lower leg. I assumed that I had been bitten by the usual black fly or mosquito that frequents our part of the woods. Or it could have been a horse fly, the population of which is still plentiful even though the mountain horse farms where my neighbors and I have made our homes have now vanished.

Before I had a chance to examine the bite, my leg was swarmed by dozens of yellow jackets, small wasps I learned that can, as my daughter used to say, "ouch you." It didn't take long—a few hours maybe—for my calf muscle to swell the size of an eggplant. The swelling, eventual redness, and muscle ache lasted nearly two weeks. And then, about a month later, the whole scenario played out again and the wasps attacked a second time. That's when I learned that yellow jackets frequently make their home in abandoned mole holes and attack from ground level, so they are pretty stealthy little creatures who show no compunction at voicing their complaints repeatedly until you pay attention. Needless to say, I learned to locate their little launch pads from a good distance, what my sensei would have called *kicking range*. In fact, my attention has become so keen for these nests that I have managed to stay safe ever since. So you'd think that would be the end of it, but my brain apparently didn't think so and went on to surprise me once again.

The surprise arrived while I was standing in my living room. Suddenly out of the corner of my eye I caught something buzzing at my head. I reflexively began flailing my arms—so much so, in fact, that had I not been in an open environment, say if I was driving on the highway instead, my actions could have been dangerous. As I jetted away from what I'd concluded was another wasp attack, I realized my assailant was only a tiny housefly. It was, in a way, humorous. Once the front of my brain got the message that the assailant was only a fly, I began to calm down, a few milliseconds after the center of my brain—my amygdala—had sent me into startle mode. The whole incident, though somewhat amusing, offered up another significant example of how out of synch emotional information processing can be.

So why do things like this occur? And is there anything you can or should do about the way you process emotional information—in particular, that which is fear-based?

The answers to these questions are rooted in some pretty primitive brain functions. Because of its evolutionary connection to survival instincts, researchers believe fear is one of the hardest emotions to control, which is why we attend to fear-based information at such high speeds. In short, your brain is primed to save your life. So again, your brain is wired to respond first and worry about accuracy later. Remember, you don't get to think about how fast you are going to run away from a dinosaur; you really have to just do it.

It may be easy to play feelings down as just feelings, but psychologists say these powerful and primitive emotional reflexes are still critical to survival. Able to fire behavioral procedures at a millisecond, emotions can help you attend to huge amounts of data at very high speeds. As such, emotions can intervene and limit the number of choices you have, making responses to incoming data timelier. On the other hand, they can also drive you away from action and into avoidance.

Emotions are responsible for feelings of relaxation, bonding, or stress. And this can be good or bad depending on the accuracy of your attention per situation.

For example, when I mistook a housefly for a wasp, the repercussions weren't serious. If, however, I had actually been the target of another wasp attack, my automatic and timely fear-based response would have helped me out of harm's way. Any attempt to have analyzed it could have been catastrophic. If, on the other hand, I had been driving on the interstate, my gut-level reaction might have created more serious problems. The difficulty is that feelings don't always point to what's best for the moment.

Is That a Tiger in the Bush, or Are You Just Glad to See Me?

Fear control is part of most martial arts training. The idea is that although you can't stop fear from entering your life, you can learn to control your reactions to it. Initially a martial artist learns to distinguish a real threat from a non-threat.

I remember the first roundhouse I ever saw flying at my head, coming in at about 75 miles an hour. My reaction must have been a sight. My anticipation of getting hit so stressed me out (which I now surmise was amplified by higher cortisol production) that it drove me to a state of total inaction. I couldn't have done anything more even if I had wanted to. I simply froze. Ironically, however, the kick missed me. But my partner, I would later learn, was hoping I would freeze—and in a way had planned on the kick missing. So when I delivered exactly what he was looking for, he made his real move, scoring a few punches instead. Over the next sequence of classes, I relived this scenario several times with my other sparring opponents. Finally my instructor had a talk with me.

"Most of the kicks that have immobilized you would have never reached you in the first place," he commented. "They are landing too far away."

He explained that, similar to many new students, my fear of getting tagged was getting the best of me. I was in a sense defeating myself. If I was going to conquer my fears, I had to be able to tell the difference between a real threat and an imagined one. And this is important. Fear is your brain's way of identifying potential trouble. You can't ignore fear or you might miss a piece of important information—sometimes there really is a tiger in the bush. So there has to be a balance. On the other hand, once you feel your fear, you can't stay afraid forever. At the right time, you have to let go, and then decide whether or not you are, in fact, faced with a real threat and then how to respond.

To help me understand, my sensei told me to mentally draw a circle around myself, of any color. The circle should be a little longer than the length of one of his kicks, a length long enough to put me out of harm's way. Then he told me to imagine another circle, of a different color, around me, a bit longer than his punches. These were my ranges.

If an opponent entered one of these ranges, I should consider his or her actions a real threat and launch an effective response. I could block, punch, kick, or perform any combination of these, as long as my responses were appropriate to the ranges I was working within. If, however, an opponent remained outside my imagined circles, even if he or she made all the noise in the world, threw any kind of menacing look or strike, taunted me, whatever, my job was to remain calm and see him as no threat.

I remember getting pretty frustrated once while sparring with my instructor. After I had thrown quite a few strikes to no avail, I commented, "You're not giving any reaction at all. I've got nothing to work with."

He flipped my comment. "You're not giving me anything to react to," he said.

With a lot of good practice and repetition, my reactions improved. But being able to assess real threats from non-threats is a skill I have to keep after even to this day and which I have learned is part of nature's way of protecting us.

Assessing threats is always difficult, but the good news is that you can get more proficient at it. Your first job, however, is to recognize and feel your fear. Then learn to let go of it and then decide what options you have for dealing with it. Whether on or off the mats, I have used this lesson to sharpen my focus and spare myself many regrettable moments.

France, 1911

There is compelling and much-written-about story brought into the mainstream by Joseph LeDoux that tells of an intriguing experiment conducted by French physician Edouard Claparede in 1911. In a report titled "Recognition and Me-ness," Claparede details the experiment, which focused on the brain's capacity for feelings of déjà vu or familiarity, and showed that certain types of recognition—such as emotional—may be rooted in some very primitive instinct. These gut feelings are similar to what he thought animals might experience when they recognize certain prey and situations without any apprehension of the past in terms of, say, dates, times, an experience's number of occurrences and so on. As the story goes, Claparede had a patient, a 47-year-old woman who, similar to the main character in the movie *Memento*, had apparently lost her ability to create any new memories. As he explained, "She forgot from one minute to the next what she was told, or the events that took place. She did not know what year, month, or day it was, though she was being told constantly."[1] One day, before meeting with his patient, Claparede carried out what he called a "curious experiment" to see if she could remember something that was purely emotional. He placed a pin between his fingers, and then as they shook hands, as per their usual greeting, he pressed the pin into her hand, and she quickly pulled away—and in a few minutes forgot it ever happened. However, the next time he extended his hand for her to shake, she quickly withdrew hers and refused.

The point to Claparede's story is that he had witnessed two different types of memory: One type that stores events and experiences for conscious recollection for a later time, and another type that can control a person's behavior without any awareness and previous learning.

Scientists refer to the first type of memory as *declarative memory*, which requires conscious recall; for example, I can remember being shocked. They refer to the second type as *implicit memory*, which is virtually unconscious and emotionally based, as demonstrated when Claparede's patient refused to shake his hand.

Okay, Let's Tear Fear Apart

Research shows that fear is part of human nature as well as virtually all animal nature. What LeDoux has found is that fear information is processed in your brain on two different pathways. He calls these pathways the *low road* and the *high road*. Low road processing bypasses the neocortex's declarative capabilities and vaults you into action quickly so you don't have to think about anything at all—a nondeclarative response, just pure reaction. In contrast, high road processing links the neocortex ability to reason into your attentional network and has the job of preventing you from making an inappropriate response. The major differences between the two roads are speed and the quality of detail provided, which influence outcomes as you move toward goals.

Here is a look at how it works. As previously mentioned, the headquarters of fear-based activity is the amygdale, and it receives both lower- and higher-level input. Sensory data (smells, tastes, the tactile feel of things, visuals, and sounds) is first processed in the brain by the thalamus and then relayed in part directly to the amygdala. The process is quick, but information is murky. On this pathway, for example, the amygdala would be unable to distinguish between a bee and a housefly or a kick that could tag you and one that would simply miss. When I think of low road information, I am reminded of old analog photocopiers and how they weren't very good at making clear generational copies (copies of copies). In fact, the further down the generational line you went, the fuzzier your copies would get. Eventually you could no longer distinguish certain details such as the difference between a "C" and an "O." So, when I try to visualize low road information, that's how I see it. Low road information processing generalizes data to the point that a stick may be indistinguishable from a snake, a BMW from a Jeep, or Barak Obama's voice from John McCain's.

But the thalamus also sends data along what LeDoux calls the high road—now involving the neocortex. The high road offers you the ability to analyze and gives you a clear and accurate account of the details. On this pathway, McCain and Obama would sound quite different.

But why does nature provide us with two seemingly redundant mechanisms for transporting fear information in the brain? And why wouldn't we have just evolved out of low road processing? Because, LeDoux reports, "The time saved by the amygdala in acting on thalamic information may be the difference between life and death. It's better to have treated a stick as a snake, than not to have responded to a possible snake."[2] On the other hand, neo-cortex involvement gives us the power to learn from, edit, and create new ways of responding to our feelings.

In a study conducted by Arnie Ohman and fellow researchers at the Karolinska Institute in Sweden, Ohman and partners found that animal-phobic people were consistently faster to locate fear-relevant targets such as snakes or spiders within a myriad of pro-jected possible targets than fear-irrelevant targets such as a flower or mushroom.[3]

Yet, as noted in the story of the tiger, distractions (in the case of the tiger story, a rabbit) can play a significant role in determin-ing the outcome of your behaviors. Interesting to Ohman's study is the effect of such distracters. When added to the mix, distracters such as flowers were able to slow down people's ability to locate fear-irrelevant targets, but not targets that were feared. This is to say that distracters may not influence the attentional speed at which you are able to locate feared targets—a significant find. In addi-tion, Ohman and partners found that people's ability to locate sad faces even in a sea of happy faces worked the same way. Negative facial expressions catch your attention faster, even amidst a crowd of happy distracters. So nice things can catch your attention and distract you from things you don't fear, but don't interrupt you when it comes to those you do fear. Wow.

For me, Ohman's work brought to mind the Amadou Diallo shooting of February 4, 1999, in which it was reported that four New York City police officers fired multiple rounds of ammuni-tion into 23-year-old Diallo, who was unarmed. The way the story goes, plainclothes officers spotted Diallo, and believing he matched the description of a (since captured) serial rapist, they approached him. Claiming that they loudly identified themselves as NYPD officers, they reported that Diallo then ran up the outside steps toward his apartment house doorway, ignoring their orders to stop and "show his hands." According to the officers, as they approached, Diallo reached into his jacket. And when he did, one of the officers believed Diallo was drawing a firearm and yelled "Gun!" to warn his colleagues. The officers opened fire on Diallo.

One has to wonder at how many junctures in such an incident alternate details—important ones—may have presented themselves, details that could have led to different choices and, perhaps, to a more peaceful solution. On the other hand, the processing speed of these life-and-death decisions is mind-boggling.

On the basis of current scientific literature, I surmise that alternate details that could have suggested other possible responses in the Diallo case may not have been able to interfere with the speed of these vital decisions. But this doesn't mean that nothing could have been done in terms of cognitive intervention. The foundation for that kind of intervention, of course, would have had to be in place much earlier, before life necessitated the need for such skill. I would deem intervention training necessary for every person in an occupation in which split-second life-and-death decisions must be made. A basic understanding of how your attentional mechanisms work can help engender intriguing new ways to intervene when life presents you with potentially hazardous automatic responses. For me, on a much lesser scale, learning a few simple bits of information about the habits of yellow jackets has helped me prevent an instant replay of what happened last summer. On a much more significant scale, an officer's learning that someone he or she may be chasing is acting on fear (amplified by a wash of hormonal activity), as the officer may be, can create a pause to examine the myriad of other data also emerging within a situation—some of which may be telling you to abort specific actions in which you are about to engage. This kind of learning may help generate clearer, more accurate assessments of high-risk situations in the future and offer more appropriate options for behavior.

The point remains: If you are looking for a snake in the grass, you can hear the sound of water, see the spray of mist, see the nylon tube and copper nozzle, and still, no matter how many of these the good distracters come into the picture you are attending to, some of which would indicate that what you are actually seeing is nothing more than a garden hose, no matter what, you are going to see a snake. And so at the end of the day, can you train your brain to operate differently? Or are you fated to be the pawn of your own neurochemical wiring?

Basic Instinct

Most dojos have various drills to help you sharpen useful basic instincts. One way to do this is to begin pushing your mental pause button on specific fear-driven responses and then redirecting your attention to the bigger picture of what is going on.

Once, my sensei brought out an enormous pair of 14-ounce boxing gloves, which are about five times the size of a normal fist. Then he paired me up with a partner in the center of the mats and told me to hold my hands behind my back. He positioned us toe-to-toe and gave my partner the gloves. My partner's job was to strike at my head using 75 percent of his normal force. I was supposed to be learning something about bobbing back and forth to avoid strikes, and, by the way, my partner was told that he was next.

Perhaps seeing the look in our eyes, our sensei took back the gloves. He told us that he was going to fire a few shots at each of us at about 25-percent torque. At the time, even a strike that light concerned me, but after taking the shots several times, I realized the gloves made it feel as though you were getting hit with a small pillow. The threat was gone, and with it my fear. Letting go of the fear helped me focus on the right things. This in turn helped me put my attention on creating the right movements required to bob away from oncoming punches. What at first had made me anxious turned out to be one of my favorite drills. To this day, I use this drill to sharpen sparring skills and to help condition unnecessary fears away.

Every year in our college dojo, I now ask my own martial arts students to identify what they fear most, in terms of self-defense. Then I assemble a group of instructors from several martial disciplines to address these concerns. One by one, little by little, we assemble techniques to eliminate everyone's qualms. We then work these techniques into visualizations to see how they can serve to conquer certain attacks before they actually present themselves on the mats—or in a real-life situation. The visualizations provide a pregame strategy so that if the attack you are working on were to occur—say on the mats—you would be ready, and even if you wind up getting tagged, at the very least you are not allowing yourself to choke or do something dysfunctional, and in short, to be defeated by your own fears.

Science and martial arts agree on this point: Your first job in dealing with fear is to feel the sum of it. Once you discover what you are afraid of, your job is to then flip through your inventory of procedures (or invent new ones) in order to identify effective ways to "take care of business," so to speak, when fear-driven situations present themselves.

EQ

Intelligence testing was invented in France in 1904, when psychologist Alfred Binet was commissioned by the French government to find a method to differentiate between children who were "intellectually normal" and those who were "inferior."[4]

Binet's test was based on what he insisted were "higher mental functions," which to him meant rational thought. Based on his work, the term *IQ* was later coined to describe a person's mental ability.

Nonetheless, most of us know from our experiences that it is hard to ignore the power emotions wield within our judgments and decisions. Still, it surprisingly took a hundred years to substantially rock the foundation Binet had established for what "intelligence" is, who has it, and who doesn't. Enter Dr. Daniel Goleman.

Goleman, whose 1994 revolutionary book, *Emotional Intelligence*, has dazzled people internationally, offers another dimension to understanding human intelligence. To this end, Goleman argues that "The very name *Homo sapiens*, the thinking species, is misleading."[5]

Indeed, there is now vast and clear research showing that when it comes to making decisions and influencing behaviors, feelings count as much as, and maybe even more than thought.

"We have gone too far," Goleman insists, "in emphasizing the value and import of the purely rational—of what IQ measures... For better or worse, intelligence can come to nothing when the emotions hold sway."[6]

Recalling that 6 a.m. scene when Isabella fantastically danced across the kitchen floor, proclaiming that she was dancing with her heart, I realize that science can now, with some real authority, map the throes of the human heart into this phenomenal field we call attention. And it is this additional element, previously considered the private realm of poets and artists, that now scientifically challenges those who subscribe to the standard that IQ is a genetic given and that regardless of your experiences in life, success and destiny will be determined solely by skills associated with IQ.

Goleman posits the question: "What factors are at play, for example, when people of high IQ flounder and those of modest IQ do surprisingly well?"[7] The difference often lies in a person's self-control, persistence, and motivation—emotional intelligence (EQ). Examples abound within our own families, workplace, schools, and personal decision-making.

Try closing your eyes for a moment. Put your attention on how you feel right now. The feeling may be subtle. You may simply feel an undercurrent of pleasantness or unpleasantness, comfort or discomfort, and the feeling may shift. But researchers believe that these subtle feelings are the program running under every decision you make and ultimately behind everything you do. In fact, can you ever remember a time when you didn't have this undercurrent of feeling? For many of us, the answer is going to be a clear no. And research shows that these feelings can have an influence on just about everything you do. EQ is about choosing how and when to attend to feelings.

Wanting to know more about the theory that had so influenced Goleman brought me to the work of University of New Hampshire psychologist Dr. John Mayer, who, with colleague Dr. Peter Salovy of Yale, formulated the theory of emotional intelligence back in 1990.

Now, somewhere toward the middle of my research, I had become suspicious that automatic, emotionally driven information could be harnessed in the world of split-second decision-making and be used to determine faster, more accurate responses. I hoped that Mayer might be able to add to this picture.

Mayer defines emotional intelligence as understanding your own feelings, as well as your empathy for the feelings of others, and the ability to regulate your own emotions such that they enhance living. Your ability to handle social relationships—which he attributes to being able to handle emotions in others—is one way to measure EQ.

Similar to all the experts in this book, John Mayer immediately struck me as a person who can walk the talk. Speaking with him is easy. He is soft-spoken and gives the impression that he is listening deeply. His attention is something you can feel, penetrating you to grasp what you are feeling and what you are thinking and welcoming you into his own mind. When you speak with him, it dawns on you that you are experiencing EQ in action. And seeing the benefits makes you eager to get yourself more emotionally intelligent.

Finally being able to speak to Dr. Mayer felt as though I was meeting the likes of any great scientific theorist one might admire. Just pick one; that's what it felt like. After all, it was he and Salovy who had in a way broadened Binet's theory that had held tight for nearly a century. Mayer is a major player in science history; it was truly an exciting experience to speak with him.

"Emotions," he explains, "are prioritizers." They are important because they can point you to something more than what's going on for you at any given moment. For example, say, you're working on the computer and the earth starts to shake, your emotions can redirect you to what's more important; that is, to get to safety. Emotions are information."[8]

Mayer refers to emotions as *hot information*, which he defines as personally relevant, declarative data with personal importance. "You might say," he explains, "Albany is the capital of New York State" (cool information) or "My and wife and I were married in Albany" (warm), or "I love living in Albany" (hot).

Emotional intelligence involves toggling your attention among all three types of information in order to achieve the best result in any given situation.

"Say you have to choose between a hanging a picture of a regular chair and an electric chair to grab people's attention in your house," Mayer explains. "Cool information just won't work. A naïve focus [as opposed to an emotionally intelligent one] is paying attention to just the hot or cool details."

Looking back I see that this can be true with regard to everything from responding to a belligerent student (or teacher) in the classroom to how one might respond to not getting a promotion he or she wanted, to pulling the trigger and firing at a suspect out of fear.

Research shows that EQ and IQ, although both measures of intelligence, are quite different. For example, purely high-IQ men and women have similar behavioral profiles. In a way they typify the comical image of, say, the professor who knows his stuff and can teach it, but take him out of the classroom and he is incapable of having a simple conversation with anyone, or the surgeon who's miraculous in the operating room, yet once her scalpels are put away, seems out of touch.

Goleman makes the case for men who are high in emotional intelligence. They, according to Goldman, are "socially poised, outgoing and cheerful, not prone to fearfulness or worried rumination...their emotional life is rich, but appropriate; they are comfortable with themselves, others, and the social universe they live in. [And emotionally intelligent women] tend to be assertive, express their feelings directly, and to feel positive about themselves; life holds meaning for them."[9]

Emotions, for good or ill, grab our attention whether we are able to deal with them intelligently or otherwise. They can rule us via some of our most primitive instincts, or we can intelligently attend to them by integrating them into our system of reasoning. It's the difference between feeling angry that your workplace parking lot has no free spaces when you are rushing to get to a 9 a.m. meeting and then doing something at the meeting you regret, or saying to yourself instead, "This is anger I am feeling, but I'm not going to let it get in the way of my meeting." Having a strong and clear sense of how you feel about life situations helps you make better decisions regarding anything from *Should I walk down this street alone at 11 p.m.?* to *Should I buy this house? Accept this job? Go out on this date? Marry this person? Engage this firearm?*

Knowing Yourself

Because of the way your brain is wired, you may have little or no control over when you are flooded with emotion or which emotions you are feeling. But you can determine how long you might remain "under this influence," as well as how to shape responses that are more aligned to goals. This brings us back to an earlier issue: your notion of self.

The hot information of emotion helps you create your idea of self and rebuild attentional procedures so that they are more functional to the person you are and want to be. In this way, emotions can be seen as contributing to a broader intelligence, which includes a more accurate understanding of self—as you view your self in past experiences, as you exist now, and in terms of what you see for your self in the future.

Self to Mayer means "self-representations of one's own personality, or it can refer to the 'I' Self or pure awareness, the execution of consciousness."

It seems Mayer's definition fits into a wide range of world literature as well as many body-mind traditions, whereas on one level self is likened to what's in your personality and on another to what these traditions refer to as the pure consciousness (and perhaps some as the soul). Whichever way you choose to look at it, within all these traditions, self comprises who you are. And as such, this brings us back to Salinger's treating self as the hub of life, insisting that if you lose touch with this part of you—your core—you stand to lose touch with everything.

But could Salinger have really known what scientists would be discovering decades after he wrote his famous book? I don't know the answer to that. There is no doubt that both would agree that it is important for us to become the captain of our own ship. From an attentional perspective this means being able to fluidly reorient your focus from what is important to the person you are at your deepest, to the details presenting themselves to you (emotional and otherwise) moment by moment, as well as what options both may offer. And because this is probably an insurmountable task, quintessential to the process is learning to prioritize.

A good friend and Hall of Fame Kung Fu grandmaster Jianye Jiang recently said to me, "I am feeling pretty good today; I think I will do more martial art work. But yesterday, no, so I stopped work early." He annunciates each word as if it is Chinese and projects each line slowly as if it were a posture in Tai Chi. "I tell students all the time," he explained, "you need to know when to slow down and when you can do more."

In our own ways, both you (the readers of this book) and I already know and practice Jianye Jiang's lesson to some extent. But Jianye's point is to make this practice a daily skill. I put his wisdom into practice when I went home that day, the day he shared it with me. Much to my delight, it greatly lightened my load and made me feel more in control and just better all around.

It's just a small lesson. But I encourage you to try Jianye's simple and yet comforting wisdom for yourself—even for just one day. You will find that the more consciously you put your attention on how you are feeling and your options for how you can use that information to finish projects and achieve goals, the better you are able to organize, plan, and accomplish tasks—and still feel good at the end of your day.

But where does emotional intelligence play in when moods turn negative? I was surprised to hear Mayer insist that negative moods and mood swings can be constructive—that was exactly the kind of surprise I was hoping he would deliver. It's all in how you choose to use hot information. You can say to yourself, "I am in a negative mood," and then use your emotion intelligently. You can do this by letting the emotion(s) point you in a functional direction. Listening to your body's emotions just as you do to its electrical waves and its chemistry, you can attend to identifying patterns evoked by specific emotions—even negative ones—and discover where those patterns lead.

Mayer explained, "You may come to realize that angry moods don't drive your creative writing, but work well for analytical work because these moods make you more critical. So, you won't be writing on angry days, but instead you may be critiquing your work or analyzing/critiquing research for use in a future manuscript."

When I thought about it I realized how much energy and critical focus I really do derive from anxious moods. Mayer had hit the proverbial nail on the head. Once aware of this use of emotion, you can opt to use even negative-feeling days constructively.

One day following our discussion I was inundated with sadness. I looked for options on how I might use my feelings constructively. I started with the idea that sadness slows me down. This made me think it would not be a day for starting a new chapter in a manuscript I was working on. I usually require a lot of energy for taking that creative leap. But, I thought, I am usually too energized or busy to look for that extra needle-in-a-haystack detail I so often want and am not always anxious to go hunting for. So I tried it high on sadness. To my surprise, the sadness not only relaxed me during this activity, but the activity then worked to get my mind off of what was bothering me in the first place. I now realize that my endocrine system had stepped up to the proverbial plate as well, rewarding me with a luxurious cascade of dopamine. Then, upon finding what I was looking for, the brain-drug rewarded me again. And when later I interjected my newly found research into my manuscript, it rewarded me yet again. The effect was synergistic: The more I discovered, the more my brain rewarded me, the more rewards I received, the better I felt, the more new research I hunted, the more plentiful the rewards, the better my overall writing became, and so on. Bottom line: Putting your attention on EQ works. Matching your moods with the right task can ramp up your ability to get specific jobs done, activate your reward system, and eventually shift you into a happier mind.

Using your emotions in this way involves a shifting of your attention from feeling an emotion and getting swept away by it, to identifying the emotion and reviewing what your options are in either holding on or letting go.

Emotional intelligence is being able to shift your attention to say, "I'll be critical today and apply my negative mood to something it is good for," or, "I am feeling good today, and so I will interact with people." Call this adaptive use.

Downward Crashing and Rose-Tinted Glasses

Once your attention attaches to a piece of hot information it tends to go after other hot information that contains the same emotional shades or feelings. This progression is called *emotional congruency*. It occurs when you feel a certain emotion and your mind immediately races to events from your past that evoked the same emotion. For example, you're feeling afraid so your mind starts popping up fearful situations from your past, forgoing happier moments. Conversely, when you are happy and flying high because, say, you just received a great promotion at work, negative events usually don't just start springing into your mind.

Scientifically speaking, emotional congruency somewhat explains why happy people seem to ride waves of happiness and depressed people spiral down. These downward moods can contaminate your attention. For example, someone can turn to you with a perfectly neutral expression while you are talking, and if your emotions are negatively charged, you may interpret the expression in a negative way.

Additionally, depressed people often use other depressing thoughts to take their mind off whatever is really bothering them. Psychologists call this a *downward crash*. According to Goleman, "People have what amounts to a set of bad-mood thoughts that come to mind more readily when they are feeling down."[10] It's like a Top 10 list that comes up automatically and offers relief in the form of distraction. What's more, it is harder to suppress this whirlpool of negative moods once they stir. The more you use negative distracters to shift focus, the more negative you become, the more you are attracted to more negativity—energizing the dive downward.

A downward crash can steal your focus. Like spinning your wheels in muck, a downward cycle is easy to get stuck in. A recent *New York Times Magazine* article reports that the danger in these cycles is that prolonged sadness can shut down your ability to think, insisting a certain brain area gets "...more active during ordinary sadness, but shuts down in people with clinical depression."[11] Some researchers believe that this brain region can literally wipe itself out if left unattended.

Not long ago, I had to undergo a laparoscopic surgery. In order to be admitted to the hospital where my surgery would take place, I had to first go through a battery of "routine" tests. Although they are common to most hospitals, anyone who has undergone such tests knows they feel anything but routine. One of the tests was an EKG. A few days before my surgery—which, by the way, I had been thinking about having for around two years—

I received a call from the hospital saying that my pre-op EKG results showed a small blip so I was being denied clearance for surgery. In order to get back on schedule, I would have to go to a cardiologist for further examination, another EKG, and a high-tech, three-dimensional ultrasound on my heart.

Like a leaf in a thunder storm, my mind whirled through my family medical history, which, in terms of cardiac problems, wasn't good. My mother died at age 53 of sudden cardiac arrest, and my father had had heart problems as well. So you can imagine the funk my mind was spinning around in.

I told the preadmission nurse that I had run 10 miles just the day before receiving the news, that I have been running five miles a day for most of my life, and that I practice and instruct martial arts avidly. I additionally have watched my diet since I was in my mid 20s. So how could this be? Things didn't add up.

"Listen, if you run 10 miles," she replied, "I think you would most likely know by now if you had a heart condition. The EKG blip is probably due to some other factor that isn't of much concern. You'll be just fine. You'll pass the tests tomorrow with flying colors." Then, to lighten my mood she bet me a $100, which of course made me laugh.

"But what's a blip?" I asked.

"It's an irregularity," she explained. "Lot's of things can cause one. The heart is a funny muscle," she responded. She repeated that I would be fine. I could tell that she didn't want me to make trouble where she really believed there wasn't any.

But my mind was looking for problems, so I asked again about the blip. This time she said that it could be caused by a "blockage." That was all I needed to hear. Now, similar to Ohman's animal-phobic clients, I chose to focus on the target of my fears. My own downward crash had begun. I had gotten what I was looking for—some really big problem to worry about to distract me from my fears about the upcoming surgery. And worry I did.

I took my attention off the nurse's confidence, which, by the way, was echoed by my doctor. And these, of course, were the very details that could have diverted some of the day's intensity. But now, looking back, I realize how our brains are hardwired to cling to such negativity if we let them. And knowing this has since helped me better understand and tolerate my own downward spirals and those of others. It has helped me identify when my brain is matching moods and to appropriately intervene. It has also helped me to better react to people around me when they get caught in the same emotional quicksand.

I remember telling myself several times not to follow my fears about the EKG, but to no avail. That evening my daughter, Isabella, asked me to hug her and carry her to bed. Dragging my feet, still wrapped up in the EKG dilemma, I made an executive decision. I forced myself to override the feeling to introvert and instead took advantage of the good diversion Isabella offered. I hugged her and robustly carried her off. I felt immediately better.

It's not easy to spin out of a downward dive when you're in one. My deepest self didn't understand the cardiology of my medical problem; I just wanted something to hold on to until my condition had been reassessed. The nurse had already given me that, telling me she didn't think there was any real danger; I just didn't want to accept it. Believing her was like reaching for a rung on a ladder that seemed out of reach. But looking at my options, I now know I didn't have to reach that rung right away. In the end, I gave myself some slack and decided to look at the facts again later, when I felt a little better. The good distraction Isabella offered was enough to focus my expectations on a better target than my fears offered: the advice given by my doctor and nurse. I put my attention there and held on. I used some meditations to help bring me to calmness. Adhering to Mayer's model, I considered the options of my fear and realized that fear had not been purposeless. Indeed, fear of ill health is what had initially motivated me to seek corrective surgery in the first place. But now my fear was getting in the way. And seeing this clearly, I took the option to let go of it. And this gave me enough peace to get through the night, and kept me open to other positive diversions in the hours to come.

The next day I woke up more rested than I would have been had I not tried to reorient my attention to more positive things. And after a battery of tests that morning, the cardiologist told me that the blip on my EKG was in fact an error and that everything was normal. This lesson will not remove all downward moods from my future, but it will affect the way I approach many of them and the influence they have over me.

Everyone is wired for emotional congruency. As such, your brain's tendency for association can help explain why, when you're happy, it seems you feel as though you are looking at the world through rose-tinted glasses, and when you're sad you manage to find more things to get sad about.

John Mayer warmly suggests, "Don't invest so much in certain perspectives. Tell yourself these things can and will change. Think: I'll feel down for a day or even a week. Then tell yourself to look at things again afterward."

Emotional Memories

Can you remember where you were when you experienced your first kiss? Or perhaps the details of a specific car or sporting accident? Or what you were doing when you first heard of the terrorist attack of 9/11? Or the details at the very moment of one of the happiest accomplishments of your life? Research shows that most people answer yes to such questions and can remember with plentiful and sharp detail. The reason for this is that emotional events have a profound affect on your memory bank. Additionally, such memories can have an ongoing affect on the emotional tone of your mind, and shade the way you attend to your day-to-day life.

Knowing something about the way you process such memories can help you use them to your benefit. Scientists say there are four types of memory that can be connected to your emotions:

The first is *declarative memory*. This is a memory that can be verbally acknowledged, meaning, if you had to, you could put the details of the experience into words for yourself or someone else.

Captured by the neocortex, declarative memory is a storage tank for declarative information. As such this kind of information engages learning and conscious awareness; for example, you touch a hot stove, you burn yourself, you learn not to touch it again. Declarative memory allows you to see the subjects of your attention in full bloom; for example, you see a yellow jacket as a wasp, not a housefly or moth. Declarative memory can call up a picture of the wasp's size, various black and yellow colorations, exact wing markings, eye shape, rapid side-to-side flight patterns, and so on.

The opposite of declarative memory is *procedural* or *nondeclarative memory*, which is essentially automated. Procedural memories kick in automatically—the formula for alphabetizing, eating with a fork and knife, riding a bike, or even habits like walking out of a room or cursing when a disagreement gets heated, or flipping someone off who cuts into your lane on the highway. Some procedural memories, such as giving someone the finger, carry a great deal of emotional weight, yet they are completely unconscious and evident only in your actions as well as upon reflection. In such cases, your brain doesn't just memorize a "task" and launch into it, but instead, combined with your primitive fight-or-flight responses, makes a procedural value judgment and then swiftly executes it without ever consulting you. Remember: some procedures surface so fast, they seem unconscious, although they are not. Nondeclarative memories are not what Freud called *repressed memories* (traumatic experiences unconsciously retained). They are virtually automated.

Your brain's next warehouse for emotional events is known as *emotional memory*, sometimes called *fear-based memory*. So again, connected to your fight-or-flight mechanism, emotional memory is fuzzy instead of stark. In this storage tank, a yellow jacket is indistinguishable from a housefly or even a piece of floating lint. The powerful effects of PTSD (post traumatic stress disorder) can in part be explained by this "lower road," dirty information. Steven Johnson writes in *Mind Open Wide*, "The amygdala of a Vietnam vet may hear an AK-47 every time a truck backfires, and every thunder storm is a carpet bombing. If the amygdala could be trained to better discriminate, these flashbacks wouldn't happen. But virtue lurks in that lack of discrimination."[12]

Just as with nearly every other aspect of human attention, there is advantage and disadvantage to this tendency of the brain. Functionally speaking the amygdala's lack of discrimination to finer and wider detail can be seen as a plus. It is, in fact, what helps a person identify all wasps, black flies, bees, and the like as threats. The amygdala's lack of discrimination cues the martial artist to lean away from a punch whether it is coming at you from the right or the left, or whether it is hooked or straight. It is what helps you identify a situation or environment you have entered as risky or safe. But at times the amygdala's fuzzy, emotional information can work against you, contaminating your ability to appropriately attend. For example, you might see a coworker's winced eyes as mocking rather than thoughtfully considering something you have just said, the sound of a lover's voice as hostile rather than happily excited, or an adversary's facial expressions as warm and loving, rather than what they really are: manipulating. Add in your moods and chemistry, and such experiences can powerfully ignite automatic procedures you've stored in memory and determine your next sequence of actions at lightening speed.

The fourth type of memory storage linked to emotional experiences is known as *flashbulb memory*, which is mostly associated with highly emotional, traumatic incidents. Flashbulb memory is made especially clear and crisp and includes not only the immediate threat, but apparently stray detail as well. For example, you might recall what would appear to be sideline details such as how bright or dark the sky was during a certain experience, how cool or warm the air, certain fragrances, sounds, and so on—all with high-resolution photographic quality. Accordingly, your brain can store images of traumatic incidents in graphic detail while seeing, hearing, and smelling a vast amount of peripheral information as well.

But note: Flashbulb memories can fool you. Dr. James V. Wertch, professor of psychology and author of *Voices of Collective Remembering*, explains why you can remember the particulars of an incident one way right after they happen and another way later. Often flashbulb memories are not from the experience itself, "but the way we rehearse the event afterward. A lot of the story gets made up; not during the event but during the retelling...it kind of grows and evolves."[13]

The terrorist attack of 9/11 is a powerful story for most Americans. As for me, my initial exposure to the event was a morning television broadcast. I remember seeing images of the attack and then rushing to describe it to my wife. At that point, my memory was fairly accurate. But today as I attempt to recall the footage I originally witnessed, I am no longer sure of its accuracy. This is because I have since seen dozens of broadcasts showing many different images of the attack, from innumerable angles and times, as well as discussed these images with many people to many different ends. My memory of the tragedy, though still sharp, is now closer to a composite picture of all these images and discussions rather than to the one I first witnessed on September 11, 2001.

What's more, tangential details of emotionally charged events may not seem significant at the time, but they are stored nonetheless, and once warehoused in your memory, they can trigger the same emotional response months, even years later.

This is why the scent of certain cologne or perfume, the tint of sunlight pouring through blinds in a certain way in a certain room, bright colors of autumn leaves on a certain street, or a certain song on your car radio can send your attention reeling into the heart of an incident you experienced years ago.

You can't help but feel and live these experiences all over again. Research indicates that such stray details can continue to push your attentional buttons for the rest of your life.

Interestingly, the brain's wiring suggests that nature doesn't seem to care much if your emotional memories are accurate 90 percent of the time or 10 percent of the time. Connected to your keenest instincts for survival, the one time you are right may, in fact, generate the exact, quick, life-saving response you need. It's not surprising that highly traumatic experiences can continue to groove their way deeper into your brain every time you remember them—orchestrating a cascade of chemicals that match those released when you first lived through the experience.

We may want to think twice, therefore, when we go home and revert to an instant replay of the day's events. If, for example, you have had a highly emotional day at the office—adrenaline and cortisol pumping through your bloodstream all day long—when you replay the details for the umpteenth time later that night, your body's automatic responses will intensify with each encore. This means that every time you imagine the dramatic scene, the more you groove it into your memory—spiked adrenaline and all—and the more automatic you make your initial response, the faster and more efficiently you will repeat it next time. Remember, the brain's knack for emotional congruity can then match your moods with equivalent memories. This brain tendency can make your whole life look like a nightmare in short order. Hanging around like a digital cookie in your field of attention, such memories compete for your focus and can work against you, surfacing at bizarre moments and driving split-second reactions that may not be in your best interests.

As a footnote, it is well documented by the scientific community that such memories can significantly contribute to a child's lack of motivation and inattention and overlap with symptoms that some caregivers want to link solely to ADHD.

But there's no panacea or magic elixir. Despite everything we might learn or how intelligent we may become, it's still not easy to push your attentional pause button, so to speak, every time you want to prevent compulsive behaviors or phobias. On a personal level, whenever someone looks at me the wrong way, I am—to this day—susceptible to being sucked into a time when someone else's look of disgust might have caused me to react in ways I wished I hadn't.

Nonetheless, no one is saying you should ignore basic instincts entirely. At the end of the day, so to speak, this kind of memory might save your life, but reminding yourself of both its accuracy as well as its lack of discrimination can help you focus on your best options per situation.

Whether you are a parent, athlete, student, policeman, politician, voter, juror, artist, businessman, or business woman, repeatedly putting your attention on such brain patterns will help sharpen your control over them. And one way you can do this is by learning to be more mindful of them as they occur.

The Art of Detachment

Martial arts teach detachment as yet another way to help you inventory (listen to) what is going on inside and outside you. And such inventory can sharpen your on-the-fly appraisals of the world.

"Detachment," my sensei insisted, "is an art unto itself." Your job, as far as he was concerned, was to empty your mind and open your focus, whether you were on or off the mats. His mantra was to then "Just go with the flow no matter what." This, according to him, would keep your mind free and spontaneous. It would allow you to change moment by moment with everything around you, which he maintained is constantly changing as well.

In martial training the key is to open your focus and keep a calm and even alertness. This gives you a chance to take inventory of your internal and external environments, as well as your opponent's.

The point is that the more you practice slipping into this state of mind the more automatic the procedure gets.

Martial arts hall of famer and author Joe Hyams writes in his book, *Zen in the Martial Arts*, "Between martial artists of the first rank, there is room for only one mistake. Before you exchange blows, several minutes may be spent in controlled patience and planning while each man respectfully observes his opponent, studying his position and stance, watching, getting ideas, and charging his energy. When one man thinks he is going to attack, his opponent may change his stance. If he has overreacted, his opponent makes note of it. This is a weakness which he will later use to his advantage."[14]

"The great masters," my sensei used to explain, "pay as much attention to pauses in which strategic considerations are made as to moments of dramatic action."

If you practice pausing to take inventory even in the middle of actions, the procedure eventually becomes automatic, at which point it is so swift it is virtually instantaneous.

Whether you are on the mats or in the middle of everyday routines, time off can be more important than time on. You learn to weigh all relevant data in your goals and then strategize the best plan to get you where you want to be—leaving enough flexibility, of course, to recalculate and restrategize as you flow.

To Be or Not to Be

Psychologists use the term *self-awareness* to refer to your ability to listen closely to and coordinate your feelings, memories, and body chemistry as you flow from one moment of life to the next. Such synchronization is made possible through your capacity to toggle your attention from one of these internal targets to the other as well as from a certain external interest to another. Self-awareness is vital to good decision-making—big or small—and ultimately to free and authentic living.

As far back as 1912, Sigmund Freud made the link between self-awareness and attention, defining self-awareness as "an evenly hovering attention" that runs steadily alongside whatever you are experiencing per moment.[15] According to Freud, this aspect of attention, which depends on one's ability to detach, has the capacity to remain neutral and objective even amidst of turbulent emotions.

Perhaps owing a lot to Freud, today's scientists define self-awareness as your ability to monitor what is happening to you both *exogenously* (internally) and *endogenously* (externally), without judgment and without censorship. As such, self-awareness is not affected by emotion.

For millennia martial arts have claimed that self-awareness is brought on by your ability to detach, and is amped up by generating higher levels of alertness and objectivity. When you are distracted, according to martial way, you must breathe—deeply. Deep breathing clears your head and energizes your focus. It's like adjusting your Internet router and immediately spiking your Wi-Fi signal from very low to excellent. As a result, according to martial teaching, you can better attend to peripheral changes in your mind and body and better coordinate these with the execution of actions. In martial arts training self-awareness is paramount.

But what happens when we disable this all-important link? Or when a person is unable to detach?

Columbia University neurologist Antonio Damasio sheds some new light on this issue. In working with *anosognosics*, individuals with damage to their emotional centers, Damasio's research has demonstrated throughout the years what can happen when a person emotionally disconnects. It is no surprise, notes Damasio, that anosognosics are profoundly impaired in planning for their future and in making decisions. As such, they are less able to foresee dire consequences to experiences and actions or suffer accordingly when they do manage to make such predictions. They are also incapable of reasonably understanding what is going on with them, what may happen to them in the future, or even how others view them. Moreover, their inability to accurately connect with their emotions leaves them unaware of these inadequacies, rendering them at times deceptively cheerful or indifferent to the situation they are in; for example, someone who loses a job or is diagnosed with cancer and continues to behave as though nothing has happened.[16] Important to attention research, Damasio's work can help neurologically explain the connection between living in an emotional vacuum and inappropriate behavior. It shows that when we are most out of touch with our emotions, we become more susceptible to inappropriate decisions, actions, and behaviors. We lose touch with our innermost self. In fact, there is plenty of research that shows discarding emotions won't make you feel better; instead, it will have the reverse affect. Like a boomerang, these emotions can fly back at you with more intensity. Conversely, disabling an emotional firewall and letting yourself feel your emotions, even if you choose to empty them from your mind afterward, will help you make predictions, match up what's going on inside and outside of you, see more options, and be more proactive.

Staying connected makes attentional sense. It is vital. Emotions help you know about yourself. They help you learn. They guide you toward actions that are good for you and your aspirations and away from those that are not.

Self-awareness, again, is central to this processing because it is the hub that connects and coordinates all of the voices taking inventory inside you, giving you on-the-go accounts of not only who you are but what you want from a specific situation, why you want this, and how these match up with the demands of your environment. Self-awareness helps you predict the success or failure of specific thoughts, feelings, and behaviors. Helping you be all that you can be, self-awareness is arguably one of your most essential skills to good decision-making and behavioral control.

The Yellow T-Shirt at a Goth Concert

Picture this: You are on your way home after work. You have taken the same route home so many times that you hardly even think about it anymore, you just put your keys in the car or jump on the same bus or subway and are off. But one day you need to make a special stop that will require a slightly different route; then, instead of doing that, you catch yourself going home the old way anyhow. The reason most of us do things like this is associated with the brain's tendency to create reflexive behaviors, which can, at times, be quite functional and, at others, not.

Enter Dr. Wythe Whiting of Washington and Lee University. Whiting is an associate professor of statistics, cognition, and evolutionary psychology. He has conducted extensive research in memory and attention, particularly with regard to changes that result in the normal aging process. My interests in reflexive behaviors, their link to emotions, and how they influence your attention as well as how they might be harnessed to boost focus and decision-making are what led me to Whiting's research.

Whiting insists that the brain power to search for and detect items in any environment is a function of two types of information processing: *top-down* and *bottom-up*.[17]

By definition, top-down processing is based on previous knowledge, expectations, and plans of action. It is able to presume things about the subject of your attention that might go beyond information contained in the subject itself. And it is capable of influencing your brain's data collection.

Speaking with Whiting is fun. He is animated, yet moves from thought to thought lightly and meticulously. He is robust and positive. And he has a knack for connecting mounds of research to instantly relatable everyday situations.

When I asked him about top-down processing, he gave me several illustrations. Say you are at a goth concert, he explained, and everyone is wearing black, and you are looking for a friend who is wearing a yellow T-shirt. Knowing that you are looking for someone in a yellow T-shirt can help you locate your friend faster. Or maybe you are looking for a piece of pink paper on a tableful of white paper. Having prior knowledge that the paper you are looking for is pink can help you to find it more quickly.[18]

This made me think of my home library. Because most of my bookshelves are often in disarray, I have become a pro at locating books by color, an example of top-down processing: I just scan for the book I know has a red-and-blue cover, and, more often than not, I find it pretty easily.

So, top-down references go to certain indicators. However, Whiting cautions, say you are looking for something blue and other blues come into the picture; the other blues will become a distraction. In fact, in such a scenario, everything blue can catch your attention and distract. So if I am looking for a book with a blue cover, a blue coffee mug I've left on one of the shelves is capable of distracting my search, ditto the blue pen, blue postcard, and blue power drink—not to mention all the other blue books. And so top-down processing doesn't always facilitate what you are attending to.

Consider the following case of mistaken identity. One day last spring I was jogging a road that runs past my home. My wife had taken both of our daughters out in their two-seat stroller for a hike along the same road. Knowing they were out, I expected to bump into them. At one point, I looked up and in the distance saw a woman pushing a two-seat stroller similar to ours. The woman had the same hair color as my wife, and she, like my wife, had her hair tied into a ponytail. As it turned out, and as you have probably guessed, this little entourage was not my family. Top-down processing had fooled me.

Research shows that memory can also play a role in top-down processing. Imagine this: You are backing your car out of a parking spot. You neglect to check behind you and almost back into an oncoming vehicle. A few days later, you are backing out of a similar parking spot. This time, you check behind you before heading out. One possible explanation for the cautionary behavior is that details from the previous incident have lodged in your memory along with an understanding that if you had checked your review mirror before backing up, the incident may have been avoided. Top-down processing, in this case, delivers.

There is a very popular illustration that shows just how much top-down processing can influence your perception. Pictured is a vase in which you might see several dolphins that appear to be swimming randomly. Affected by what you already know, believe, and expect, you may see something different than another person when you first look at the figures in the illustration. If, say, your attention goes to other detail in the picture, you may not see the dolphins at all. You might instead see two adults, a man and a woman, embraced intimately. It has been reported that children who have yet to experience adult intimacy almost always see the dolphins and miss seeing the two embraced adults—even when told to look for them.[19]

Top-down processing is powerful. It not only biases the way you collect information but can ultimately bias your perceptions as well.

Bottom-up processing is the other type of information processing, with powerful attentional significance as well. It works as its name suggests—from ground level up. It is what happens when you are in the middle of a meeting and the lights unexpectedly go out, and wherever your attention was, it suddenly isn't anymore. Whiting explains, in such an instance, your attention moves from one place to another as if you have no choice.

Bottom-up processing allows interpretations to emerge from the data you are inventorying (internally or externally) rather than from schematics (plans) and expectations already in your memory. The operative word is *emerge*.

In bottom-up processing, the data itself provides your guidance. As such this kind of processing is most efficient when the features of the target of your attention are distinct from the features of nontargets—like a black tire on a sandy beach.[20] Bottom-up processing happens when you move your attention from the television show you are watching to the power that has suddenly gone off. In contrast, top-down processing happens when you turn on a mental detection map to locate targeted items that are not so obviously distinct. It plays in, for example, as soon as you ask *why* the power has just gone off.

Putting an evolutionary lens onto the world of brain science, Whiting says that evolution does not allow us to keep things that are not functional. And this, he explains, is the case with top-down and bottom-up processing; in other words, there is a time and place for both.

Generally speaking, neither form of processing is better than the other. When something relevant happens in our environment that requires our immediate attention, such as a dangerous snake appearing in the grass, we should be able to fall back on bottom-up processing and let fear drive us out of harm's way. On the other hand, you can't run from everything that approaches you. And top-down information can provide a schematic to help you decide what is dangerous and what isn't—what is an accident about to happen and what is a non-threat.

On a personal note, I recently found myself about to finalize a new piece of research I had been working on for some time. It was late afternoon and the campus seemed deserted. I was probably into the 11th hour of my project with not much time left to finish. Nonetheless, I decided to step out of the office for a moment to get a little fresh air. I hadn't been outside very long at all when a colleague suddenly came over and started a conversation. She had a lot to say, and the conversation was getting on. Maybe it was because of all the writing I'd been doing on attention that it seemed funny that in the middle of an important research project I should be so easily distracted. I could feel my top-down biases activating, tagging the conversation as an interruption, and as irrelevant. I started looking for an opportunity to skip out of it. I remembered a similar conversation my colleague and I had had earlier in the year and felt myself getting annoyed. But then something else happened—again, probably spurred by my recent attention research. I knew that just recognizing the behavioral patterns bubbling up into my awareness wouldn't make them go away. So I decided to try a harmless experiment, if only to see if I could make my own neural apparatus work.

I began by detaching, and tried to override the biases I was feeling. *Why not?* I thought. The worst thing that could happen was that I'd lose a little time and have to pick up my work again the next day. I took an inventory of what was going on inside of me. I could feel the subtle rush of adrenaline, the annoyance, and the memories I'd already begun dredging up. I told myself to say no to the guided missile my attention had become, and instead of letting it pull my strings, so to speak, I stepped back, took a breath, and acknowledged what I wanted from the situation. What I really wanted was to humor myself and see where things would naturally go if I just let them. I let my attention just hover as objectively as I could. And then, without any coaxing, my colleague delivered a piece of information that ironically would put the frosting on the research project I was deadlining on. All I needed was to ask her to talk just a little more—which she, of course, was happy to do. Interestingly, the amount of time we'd spent getting to that sweet place was nothing compared to the time her advice was going to save me in the coming hours.

My little experiment had taught me that the worlds of top-down and bottom-up processing can be bridged. But it also reminded me that you have to be careful. Top-down biases can close doors to important life opportunities. You can, however, learn to toggle between the two—which, in my little experiment, worked magic.

Priming

Consider this: You walk into a colleague's office and a randomly placed briefcase begins to influence the way you see the world. Or you are handed a pen and asked to fill out a questionnaire, and, unbeknown to you, the pen asserts an influence over your behavior, making you more aggressive, competitive, and even greedy. Sounds like science fiction. Well, its old knowledge that the way a person outfits an office or home can characterize that person. But new research shows that such items can also drive your attention and even influence your actions. Psychologists call this effect *priming*.

By definition, *priming* refers to the unconscious activation of memories or parts of memories just before carrying out a task. A classic experiment shows how this works: In the test, participants are generally asked to read a list of words that contains a term such as, say, *manager*. Then later, they are asked to complete the word *manag*. The wordlist they attended to earlier functions as a prime and thus influences many people to respond with the word *manager*.

Priming can also work by association. According to Dr. Tram Neill, you can identify a word such as *nurse* from a string of letters more quickly if you have recently used or responded to a word such as *doctor*. On the other hand, if you intentionally ignore or block a piece of information, your subsequent responses to related information may actually be slower or less accurate than they would be to new data. This effect is called *negative priming*.[21]

"Pretty much everything can be primed," says Dr. John Bargh of Yale University. "Mention the word *library* and people tend to speak more quietly. Put a photo of a loved one on your desk and you start behaving as if they were physically with you."[22]

Bargh likens priming to a hypnoidal state, in which memories, objects, attitudes, and words can catch your attention and thus drive your behavior. For example, in one study he found that when subjects (who had, at an earlier time, wanted to make their moms proud) were asked to think about their mothers, they were able to out-perform others in specific tasks.

It's enough to make you think twice before putting that new painting on your wall or easy chair in your den, or who you think about before doing an important job.

Psychologists say that people can even be primed to think of themselves as smart or not, and that such associations can lead to success or failure. In his book, *Blink*, Malcolm Gladwell offers an overview of a test conducted by psychologists Claude Steel and Joshua Aronson. The test involved African American college students and 20 questions taken from the Graduate Record Examination: "When students were asked to identify race on a pretest questionnaire, that simple act was sufficient to prime them with the negative stereotypes associated with African American academic achievement—and the number they got right was cut in half."

What's more, when Aronson asked the students involved in his test if they thought anything lowered their performance, they would say no. When asked if it bothered them that he asked them to indicate their race, they said, "No...you know, I just don't think I am smart enough to be here."[23]

But just how subtle can primes get? Can even briefcases and pens prime your attention and influence your behavior? Can everyday objects actually make a person more aggressive, competitive, and greedy?

Psychologist Christian Wheeler, a professor and honored scholar at Stanford University, has carried out numerous studies in which he exposed individuals to such objects to see how much influence they could have on people. When I spoke with Wheeler, he outlined one such experiment.

"Well, so," he began, "this experiment was designed to test the idea that objects in the environment can activate mental associations that can influence our perceptions and behavior. The context of the experiment was that we told people they were going to play a game with another person; it was an economic game, and they believed that they were in a position to receive some money and to propose a division of that money between themselves and another person. And the game in the briefcase study was a standard ultimatum game; it's something commonly used in economics."[24] Confident and clear, Dr. Wheeler spoke as if he has considered the details of the experiment many times, going over each layer with me systematically. It was experiments such as this that earned him the 2008–2009 Ormand Family Faculty Scholar at Stanford, which emphasizes profound, frontier American scholarship.

"The basic idea," Wheeler continued, "is that we gave participants $10 and we said, you can propose any division of this $10 that you like: you can keep all $10 for yourself, give all $10 to the other person, or anything in between; the only catch is that if the other person rejects your offer neither one of you gets anything."

"So the person, if you're too greedy, could say forget it, and then neither one of you gets anything," I said.

"Right," said Wheeler. "In reality, in this experiment there was no other person in the other room. But what we were interested in is simply the allocations that they made and how essentially greedy they were going to be. And what we manipulated were the objects in the room."

So in one condition, Wheeler took the questionnaires out of a black briefcase and participants completed their questionnaires with a silver-barreled executive-style pen, and when they were finished with their questionnaires, they put them in a black executive portfolio (this was the "business objects" condition). As for the other condition randomly assigned to participants, he took the questionnaires out of a black backpack and they completed the questionnaires with a #2 pencil and then put them in a cardboard box when they finished.

"These objects were designed pretty neutral," Wheeler explained. "So the idea was that the business objects would activate mental constructs associated with the business world, and the relevant one here would be competition, and that that would influence the allocations that people made in the game. And it did. People kept more of the money for themselves in the business-objects condition than in the neutral-objects condition."

Some pretty significant behaviors driven by some fairly simple objects, I thought.

Wheeler's mood lightened, as if he were about to give away the scoop on how to perform a dazzling magic trick, except this wasn't really magic—in the technical sense, anyway. He took a breath and nonchalantly reported (suggesting this is simply just the way it is), "Participants are clearly aware of objects in the room. If you ask them, 'Did you notice a briefcase or a pen?' they will say yes. But what they are unaware of is that those objects have any influence on their behavior, and so if you ask them why they made the allocations they did, no one will refer to the objects as one of those reasons. If you ask them specifically—you know there were a number of objects in the room that could influence people's behavior—'Did that object have any influence over your allocations?'—everyone says no. **So, in this case, they are aware of the stimuli, but they are not aware that the stimuli are activating the construct, in this situation, of competitiveness, or that that has any influence on their judgments or behaviors."**

Wheeler insists the whole thing with priming is that "it is activating specific mental contents and memory that can shape the things you pay attention to as well as the way you interpret things." What's more, the influences of priming can continue for a time after your initial exposure. Wheeler cited another part of his business objects study in which people read about an ambiguous scenario, yet perceived the scenario to be more competitive if they'd already viewed the business objects.

Indeed, we are a lot more susceptible to the affects of priming than we may realize. The point is, says Wheeler, such influences "can shape the direction of our intention and shape the types of actions we engage in." What's more, he says, "Anything in your environment can activate mental constructs without your awareness."

But can you ever become aware of what's priming you? And is it possible to use primes to boost your brain power?

"*Priming* by definition involves a people's lack of awareness of these things [what's priming them]," says Wheeler.

Nonetheless, many people have learned to regulate addiction to things such as smoking, caffeine, sugars, and so on, as well as urges toward more disconcerting dependencies and behaviors. So, at some level, it would seem that they are able to connect a few of the proverbial dots.

"The fact that people happen to be unaware in our studies doesn't mean that they would necessarily *have to be* unaware," says

Wheeler. He thinks about this for a moment, then continues, "For example, if you were to warn people before they came into the room that the objects in this room might influence your judgment or something, people may become attuned to those objects and try to eliminate their influence on their judgment."

Other research indicates that you can learn to recognize cues or primes that signal availability for natural incentives through memory; in other words, you may think, *I did such and such before and it served me well.* Students, for instance, learn that if they can stay interested in a class or lecture and take good notes, they can achieve higher grades. A person who is trying to lead a sober lifestyle can immerse himself in an environment that primes and rewards sobriety. If you are trying to become proficient in sporting, art, parenting, and so on, you can surround yourself in environments, using everyday sights, smells, sounds, and encounters, that will activate behaviors conducive to your goals. What's important to note is that putting your attention on how specific people, places, and things affect you—even in the subtlest of ways—helps you discover which ones are triggering positive primes and which are disruptive.

Catching Someone Else's Emotions

Consider this: Have you ever walked into a room and felt as though someone was sucking the energy right out of you before either of you ever had the chance to utter a word? Or what is it that makes us get so wrapped up in movies, novels, and arts such as music and dance? Why do we get so emotional by merely observing other human beings?

Psychologists refer to this brain tendency as *empathy*. They tell us that without it we wouldn't be able to connect with the world in which we live. And it is this brain circuit, which science now tells us is wired into our cells, that helps us look at people in our world and see more than just another face. Empathy is what helps us experience what's under another person's skin—feel what he or she is feeling, share parts of our own mind, and sometimes bond.

Noted by every spiritual tradition on the planet, our ability to empathize helps us establish happy, peaceful and successful actions wherever we go. But how does this so often talked about, yet sometimes mysterious, brainpower work?

Dr. Donald Pfaff, professor and head of the Laboratory of Neurology and Behavior at The Rockefeller University, offers an explanation. Pfaff is an all-star brain scientist known in the neuroworld for discovering the exact cellular targets for steroid hormones in the brain. His recent book, *The Neuroscience of Fair Play: Why We (Usually) Follow the Golden Rule*, theorizes that empathy can prevent us from harming others as well as lead us to do good. Pfaff's theory is that empathy is rooted in hard science. And as such he believes it can open a whole new dimension to understanding and utilizing the empathic capabilities that are everyone's birthright.

When Pfaff and I spoke, I asked him the question that had been burning in my mind ever since I had came across his terrifically enlightening book: What did he mean exactly when he wrote that we—our brains—are wired for the golden rule?

"What it was intended to mean," Pfaff explained, "was that, without assuming any special cognitive powers, that our neural circuitry was set up to allow us to see ourselves in the position of the other person and the other person in the position of ourselves. And therefore, not to do to that person what shouldn't be done and what we wouldn't want done with ourselves."[25]

Pfaff is fervent about his work. He is congenial and carefully considers what he is about to say, then lays it out, in a burst of dazzling information—quickly, yes, but also wanting you to understand, constantly checking to see that that you are still "with him." And if you are not, he'll gently get you there with more examples and crystal-clear logic.

"The theory," he noted, "takes as an assumption that we can recognize ourselves as different from other things in the world." He paused and thought about what he was going to say next. Then continued, "And having said that, I would say the book [*Fair Play*], in my current thinking since the book, sort of splits off into two parts—one is more motor and the other is more sensory."

The motor part he referred to starts with a discussion of *corollary discharge*, which he explains says that "We are—our selves are— the persons whose motor behavior we can predict and remember, meaning that I recognize myself as the person who, if I am about to shift my eyeballs to the right, I know that's going to happen and I have a motor record of it through this corollary discharge. Or if I'm willfully to lift my leg or any other movement, that I can both anticipate it and have the muscle memory of it."

This says Pfaff has a very concrete definition of self, not, as he puts it "as some ethereal being but instead as a motor automation."

Trying to visualize his point even as I write this book, I reach for a glass of water. If I strengthen my focus, just a little, I can develop a mental picture of myself doing it, but the picture runs a little blurry in my head. Nonetheless, I can see myself doing it and I can also recall the image. Amusingly the image I am able to make in my mind in a way resembles a hologram.

There is another side to self, however, that Pfaff says is more on the sensory side. This element of self can allow a person to envision himself in a way that's different from the way he envisions other people. It is an internal representation of a sort that's different from just looking at another person's image or photograph and recognizing the person. "So it's probably a pre-motor cortex function" says Pfaff. "And again, it's almost a motor memory, but it's a looking-at-my-self-from-without, so to speak."

This creates an almost Zen-like image for me. It reminds me of this sort of uncanny ability we have to look at ourselves from both within and without. For example, say I am at home and my daughter's friends are coming over to visit and I know they can get pretty energized, so I decide to move a few things such as, say, my laptop computer, which is on the end table in the living room, back into my office, to keep it safe. When I am doing this self-consciously, if I'm doing it thoughtfully, then I'm envisioning myself putting the computer away so that it will be safe. The image that comes to mind, for me, is that it is like looking at an automation (hologram) of myself, only knowing what is going on both outside the image and inside as well.

According to Pfaff, "This ability to claim one's own reflected image is important not only for the recognition of self, but also for the ability to understand and imitate others."[26] And it seems that we are hardwired to do just that.

Science tells us new research can give us a neurological explanation for this capacity to empathize with others. Most important to this research is a circuit of brain cells found on both sides of the brain called *mirror neurons*. These neurons have the remarkable power to help us catch people's emotions.

Pfaff argues that mirror neurons must help in the empathic process, but he says that his theory in *Fair Play* "doesn't depend absolutely on them. My theory," he emphasizes, "enjoys them because it makes it easier to say that we're wired for reciprocity with these neurons, mirror neurons, but the theory's much more abstract than that and says that anything that blurs two images, whether it's mirror neurons or something else, would do the job. By the way," he asked, "do you know how they [mirror neurons] were discovered?"

As I understood the story, an Italian scientist named Giacomo Rizzolatti had been conducting an experiment that involved monitoring a monkey's brain when he discovered the neurons. Some people in the science community were hailing the find as the 21st century's equivalent to the discovery of DNA.

Pfaff questioned, "And the cup of coffee? Did you hear about that?"

"No," I responded curiously. "I don't know about that."

I had the feeling that I was about to hear a behind-the-scenes account of one of the most dazzling discoveries in recent brain science. Pfaff told the story with enthusiasm. I could tell he really liked it.

The way the story goes, Rizzolatti and partners were recording from a monkey's pre-motor area. "There's the motor cortex, and in front of the motor cortex going to the anterior there is the pre-motor cortex," Pfaff explained, and continued, "and these two Italian scientists were recording from a neuron that responded— would fire action potentials—when the monkey held its arm out in front of it. And then it was time for lunch. So they went across the room in the same room where the monkey was and the monkey could see them [his voice goes up excitedly], and one of the guys suddenly notices that the neuron over there was firing, but the monkey was not holding his arm up in that position. The monkey was looking at him, the experimenter, holding a cup of coffee, and at that point he thought—I don't know how you say 'holy cow' in Italian—but *holy cow, this monkey is responding to my arm position*, the experimenter's arm position, and of course it was all sweetness and light after that."

What had astonished the scientists was that the monkey hadn't moved at all. The human had moved. To this particular neuron, there was no difference between watching somebody do something and doing it yourself. Just seeing someone else do something was good enough to fire it. These neurons, which scientists had concluded were involved in the coordination of the monkey's personal actions, were also connected to the actions of others.

Researchers finally realized that the whole mirror phenomenon wasn't just about monkeys, but that these circuits could guide and mature human attention as well. At first, a lot of research focused on how these neurons helped people learn, especially in terms of new motor skills (or improving existing ones). For example, infants watch you raise a hand, and they raise theirs, copying your movement. You move your hand forward, they do the same, and you can eventually teach them to play high-five. When we get older, and we learn the right way to grip the steering wheel, strum a guitar, kick a soccer ball, or hug a person intimately, we get help from the same mirroring system.

Scientists also believe that mirror neurons can help extend our self-awareness to include the feelings of others by making it possible to feel other people's joy or grief, pleasure or displeasure, as if it were actually happening to you. This, then, gives you a better grip on that person's intentions as well as to the consequences of his or her actions.

Targeting your attention on what people around you mirror back will show you what you are putting out and how it is affecting others. It can show you whether your actions are in synch with your goals.

This knowledge can help you make better choices about what actions you need to keep and which you may want to change. It helps establish peace and harmony in your life. And as with all other attentional skills, the more you practice, the better you get at it.

Consider the following example: You walk into the kitchen after a bad day and without thinking throw your keys on the countertop. All your partner has to do is hear the sound of the keys hitting the countertop and he or she will begin to experience your anger, mirroring it back to you. Remember, each time the emotion feeds back and forth between you, it can also intensify, activating your body chemistry as well as memories. When unwanted emotions and memories begin to loop, they spike and can soon become quite troublesome, and sometimes even dangerous.

A small change in how you process things can make all the difference in the world. Let's play the previous scenario another way: You arrive home. You know you have had a bad day and feel dreadful so you compensate by making yourself more aware of your actions, especially your body language and your words. You concentrate on moving and speaking more slowly, more softly, and more thoughtfully. You try to see your actions from outside and inside as well. You consider your emotional options as you take inventory. You are careful to stay calm, and so you can catch yourself about to throw the keys. At this juncture, you consciously choose to gently place the keys on the countertop, instead of throwing them. You try reading your partner's body language until you see an appropriate moment to describe your day. You decide what you want your partner to understand from the story you are about to tell and what you want in return. You consider how these will fit into the big picture of your relationship. You decide to tell the story, using these goals as your guide. You remind yourself that life has suddenly given you an opportunity to affiliate rather than alienate at the end of an otherwise rough day.

What we do and what we feel is connected to what other people are feeling and vice versa. You can learn to use your attention's executive functions to help you press pause more often—even in a split-second decision. This can give you more choice in what is going on in your life and what you are being invited into. And you can ultimately choose more strategically.

The Subway Hero

Empathy has a lot to do with getting and maintaining control.... It is a vital growth step because it provides you more information with which to gauge your responses as you work toward daily goals.
—Frank Vellutino

On January 2, 2007, Wesley Autrey became an international hero. Autrey, a 51-year-old African American construction worker and former Navy veteran saved a young Caucasian man who had apparently suffered a seizure and fallen onto the subway tracks in Manhattan by jumping onto the tracks himself and pushing them both between the rails, underneath an oncoming train. If that's not enough, imagine this: Autrey's two daughters who were with him watched as their father dared the heroic rescue.

What was so amazing was that Autrey made his decision to get involved in a flashing second: leaping onto the tracks and laying on top of the young man's body to shelter him as five subway cars screeched over them. And perhaps just as fascinating, when it was all over and the crowd cheered, this is what Autrey thought to say: "We're okay...I've got two daughters up there. Let 'em know their father's okay!"[27] His thoughts were not self-aggrandizing or platitudinous. They were instead the caring and protective and empathetic thoughts of a father.

"I don't feel like I did something spectacular," Autrey commented. "I just saw someone who needed help and did what I felt was right."

And so the whole scene was a lot about empathy—for 20-year-old Carmen Hollopeter, the young man whose life Autrey had saved, and for his daughters. Writing of Autrey's heroism, Dr. Pfaff has commented that "Mr. Autrey's brain must have instantly achieved an identity between self-image and the image of the victim who fell in front of the subway train."[28] And so he wanted to help Hollopeter because that's what Autrey would have wanted in the same situation. But how did Autrey know what to do?

Autrey claimed he had to decide what to do in a split second. Interestingly, he credited all his years of experience as a construction worker with helping him gauge whether there would be enough space for the subway trains to pass over him and Hollopeter. But was there anything else going on in that mind about to leap into one of the most famous altruistic deeds in history?

There was. According to Pfaff, Autrey attended in a way that demonstrates the prosocial caring that Pfaff hypothesizes normally develops from parental and familial love. In fact, Autrey himself had said afterward, "I didn't want the man's body to get run over. I didn't want my daughters to see that." Again, his thoughts went to his daughters. This kind of empathy, research indicates, is linked to some very primitive survival tendencies exhibited by males—

especially in the protection of their offspring. And according to Pfaff, these are supported by hormones such as testosterone and vasopressin to amplify the aggression required for the execution of such protective acts.

I find it dazzling to imagine what might have been going on in Autrey's head when he performed such an incredible act of heroism. First, I envision an empathic mechanism I have come to believe all human brains contain: all circuits wired for empathy firing brightly, putting Autrey's attention smack in the mind and body of a fellow human in need; both he and Hollopeter, in a sense, neurologically melded together in this moment in time, and then, in a split-second decision, Autrey launches to assist, accompanied by a series of life-saving attentional procedures (perhaps accrued from years of construction work); all of these firing in milliseconds to the cascade of testosterone and vasopressin streaming through Autrey's blood to facilitate him, chemically linking him to selfless, protective acts carried out by fathers throughout history.

Wesley Autrey is an American hero. And although we will probably never be in a position to use our own bodies to shelter other people from an oncoming subway train, we can benefit from learning how to regulate the same attentional mechanisms that triggered in Autrey's brain and use them to help facilitate our own daily lives. Let's see how.

SELF-REGULATION

*Without self control, we can have the strongest of
motivations and set the highest of goals, yet we
will invariably get sidetracked...*
—Maggie Jackson, author of *Distracted*

Here Comes Everybody

Picture this: It is Thanksgiving Day. You are expecting guests to celebrate the holiday with you. You have been preparing food all morning, and your home is feeling and looking quite lovely. You are a bit anxious. It is almost time for company to arrive. Suddenly you hear the doorbell ring. You look out the window and a good number of guests have arrived all at once, and they are holding armfuls of luscious foods. You begin to greet people, and more guests arrive, also carrying goodies with them. It would be easy to see the situation as a bit overwhelming and chaotic (and you might, for a moment, because the scenario is not something you deal with every day). You have, however, planned the celebration for weeks, and so you do have some pre-sense (*schema*) of how you want things to go. Besides, you are caught in all the excitement. It's going to be a terrific party, you think. Your memory is full of schemas from other successful parties you have hosted. So when someone asks, "Where do you want this?" you simply say, "What is it?" "Hors d'oeuvres," you're told. "Over there," you motion toward the kitchen counter, remembering that's where they went last year and that worked out well. "And what about these?" someone else asks. "And this?" As if it is the most natural thing in the world, you begin to slip into "party management mode" and begin directing: desserts over here. Beverages over there. Veggies in there. Some of the information you receive conflicts with other information you may have in mind: "How about we put salads over here with the veggies?" someone recommends. But you suggest the dining room instead, "Actually there is a whole table in there just for all the different salads." And sometimes you correct a managerial error: "Sorry but I don't know what I was thinking. This is probably a better place for that." Or someone's suggestions may not fit your schema, but they work—maybe even better than what you have planned: "That's not what I had in mind," you find yourself saying, "but I like your idea better." And even though guests may keep coming in after the initial rush, and there is an awful lot of competing information coming at you from all fronts, you have automatically narrowed your focus to "welcoming guests and food management," and it is all, in the end, easily doable.

I like using Thanksgiving Day as a metaphor for how we can naturally supervise large amounts of information that shape what we think and do and yet manage to remain calm and focused as we move—with some sense of mindfulness and self-awareness— toward our goals. When you actually stop to think about it, you can manage quite a bit of information at any given moment. Whether you are inventorying the language of hormones or feelings, whether your goal is social, professional, emotional, or athletic, your ability to listen to and process incoming data is fantastic.

Our "guests," in terms of attention-building, are: thoughts, feelings, emotions, hormones, memories, and constellations of external data—all capable of activating procedures that will successfully (or not) guide you through your next series of actions.

The managing process, similar to Thanksgiving Day, is a matter of toggling your attention from external to internal information and looking for a match. Ultimately you can choose to listen to, work with, and direct this data so that you can take advantage of the best options it offers. Or you can let your preprogrammed responses kick in and take over. You can also choose both ways to proceed. And bear in mind, you always have the option to ignore data as irrelevant as well.

It sounds overwhelming, and if you tried to take control of every minute detail of your life this way, it would be. Realistically, however, most of us would opt out of doing such a thing. For one, it would defeat the very point of having automatic functions—which is to provide you with more brainpower for other things you may need to be processing and consciously controlling. But on the other hand, you don't want to always succumb to your default settings either. There is plenty you can do to train your attention to take carefully planned, high-speed control of life's important moments to assure you have some say in how they turn out.

Your Attention's CEO

Science tells us that as humans we are able to regulate our thoughts, emotions, and actions to a greater extent than other primates. Indeed, nature has wired us with the capacity to identify priority moments in our lives and make executive decisions about them. We can choose, for example, to hold off on something we want for something we can predict is better down the line. We can make plans, we can avoid distractions, and we can work toward goals. What makes this all possible is your executive (or supervisory) attention functions.

Much the same as an executive might examine details related to an entrepreneurial decision, your executive attention can target your focus to appropriate internal and external details and make goal-related decisions accordingly. In this way, executive attention is closely connected to intention or willpower.

Developmentally, human infants have the longest period of dependence upon caregivers of any mammal. Nonetheless, and perhaps as a way of controlling distress, we begin sparking executive attention functions within the first year of life.

During the first three months of infancy, caregivers usually say they will try to regulate distress by holding or rocking the infant. Interestingly, after the third month many caregivers, especially in the Western cultures, try to distract infants by guiding their attention to other stimuli. When the infants attend, they are often calmed.[1] Could this be seen as resulting from a primitive distress management system? Many psychologists think so. In fact, current literature shows that the difference between the adult and the child is in the unfolding of executive functions, which, for the child, begins with distress management and then operates at higher, more willful attentional levels in the second year of life.[2]

As you advance into adulthood your executive attention matures and manifests in the ability to resolve conflicts, correct errors, and plan new actions.[3] It becomes necessary in situations in which routine or automatic processes are inadequate—anything from sparring on the mats to welcoming Thanksgiving guests, to arriving at work and having to deal with an unexpected issue. Importantly, executive attention can regulate a variety of networks, including emotional responses and sensory information, and it is essential for most other skills, as well as for academic and social performance. The good news is that researchers find that executive attention is a trainable mechanism with no apparent ceiling. And this is important because the clinical message is this: **There is no end to how much attentional brainpower you can build.**[4]

And this brings us to what everything in this book has thus far led up to: Your capacity for self-regulation.

Self-Regulation

Self-regulation has become an area of rapidly growing interest in a variety of literatures that range from retraining your brain, to healthier, happier living, and to professional and interpersonal success at all levels. And for the vast majority of us, self-regulation is really the ultimate game in attention training. Perhaps the best reason for this is that it works. And there is much clinical support to prove it.

But what exactly is self-regulation? In general, the term refers to exercising control over various elements involved in achieving and/or maintaining one's daily goals. More specifically, self-regulation is the management of conscious and/or automatic processes that influence your attention, thoughts, emotions, memory, blood chemistry, and other physiological functions, motivations, behaviors, and goal performance. To this end, most researchers believe that self-regulation can be a conscious, volitional act involving your executive attentional functions.

Dr. James Diefendorff's work in the area self-regulation is inspiring and enlightening. Diefendorff, a psychologist at the University of Akron, writes extensively about the links between self-regulation and attention, and especially in what things tend to make the self-regulating processes work. When we spoke, Diefendorff told me that he has a passion for studying why people do things and how we can use our attentional skills to stay motivated through time as well as to help manage our cognitive resources.

"We have distractions of all sorts that can interrupt our ongoing thought processes," Diefendorff explains. "We even have other goals and emotions that can try to gain access to our attention and take control of it. So understanding how to keep those things from interrupting you is critical to how you maneuver through your daily life."[5]

One way to keep things from interrupting is to set goals and intentionally turn off distracting information or mark it irrelevant. Diefendorff reports that "Individuals who can effectively initiate action toward goals [action-oriented goals] and better block out non-goal-relevant information have higher levels of perceived self-regulatory success."[6]

The point is that if you start thinking about a goal and how (when, why, where, and so on) you are going to achieve it, the better you will be at turning off irrelevant, distracting information when it exhibits itself along the way.

"Our research," Diefendorff explained, "basically shows that people who exhibit less cognitive inhibition processes—so, basic cognitive functioning with regard to being able to ignore distractive information—are less effective at self-managing a lot of different life demands including work, health, emotion regulation, and academic as well. People who are not able to suppress as effectively have more difficulties."

Thus the better your inhibition—that is, your ability to block or mark certain information as irrelevant to task requirements—the more you can keep distractions out of your working memory, making it more efficient as you approach your goals. But how much regulation can you really achieve through sheer willpower? Researchers believe that the answer to this, depending on the task, can be a lot.

"I think it's partly volitional," says Diefendorff. "Some of it is hardwired; it's just biological. But I think that you can, if motivated; I think the desire to self-regulate can enhance your tendencies to do so. A lot of where your motivation is going to have its effect is through more conscious, more deliberate strategies—and you may have to work at such things as:

- Understanding what kinds of circumstances are going to distract you and preventing those circumstances from occurring.

- Understanding how to interpret something such as an error or a failure in a more positive way so you don't become immersed in thoughts about this negative state you're in.

- Understanding how to keep your attention focused through more deliberate, conscious activities.

That's where I think motivation and willpower come into play."

Diefendorff insists that whenever you are experiencing a correction or an error that there are two ways you can interpret it: "Basically you can think about these as a either a threat or an opportunity," he explains. "You can say, well, an error may signal that I am no good at something, which can lead to lots of debilitating, negative thoughts about yourself—or, an error [he says with emphasis] could signal this is an opportunity to master whatever you're working on, to become more proficient at it, which would prevent those negative emotions, which would subsequently keep you focused on the goal you're striving for."

There is an ancient martial arts tenet that evolves from the notion of going with the flow. The idea is that every movement of life contains opportunity somewhere within it. It is a lesson that is difficult to master—at first. This is because the novice often sees a foiled endeavor as a failure, and his or her next series of feelings, thoughts, and actions are guided by that conclusion. One possible explanation for this reaction is the novice's giving so much attention to controlling an opponent's behavior instead of accepting it and putting his attention instead on controlling (seeing, activating, and inhibiting) his own options. For example, say a novice launches a technique that relies on two rapid strikes. The first strike gets blocked, eliminating the possibility of the second strike he had in mind. Beginners often become discombobulated at this point (out of disappointment or anger or some other negative emotion), and in the split second during which they disengage, are successfully countered by their opponent. Detrimental emotions, memories, blood chemistry, and procedures are kicking in and contaminating a better response.

Martial artists of high rank usually become much more adept at activating relevant data and inhibiting irrelevant data, pretty much on-the-fly, though they sometimes practice visualizing such moments from past experiences to help groove strategies into their memory so it will be available later. The more seasoned player won't disengage at a foiled strike—or even see the foil as an error. Instead she may see opportunity in the "new movement" and gracefully roll right over the top of her opponent's block, straight into an armlock, judo-throwing him as if it was all meant to happen just that way.

Diefendorff pointed to an area of research he identifies as *error management training*, which he explains "deals with training employees how to perform a task. The traditional perspective is that errors are bad. That whenever you learn how to do something, practice makes perfect. And that you don't want to make errors while you are learning."

"Probably anything from writing a term paper to driving a car or getting along with your partner," I submitted.

"That's right," he responded. "I think that's the traditional notion. But errors, as a lot of us know intuitively, can be beneficial too."

So if you can learn to reinterpret an error not as a threat to your ego, but as an opportunity to become more proficient at something, you've wiped out the possibility of negative emotion occurring whenever you experience error.

"But that's not always feasible," explained Diefendorff. "Sometimes errors really are problematic, but I think that in a lot of situations where you have a choice about how to interpret negative information or information that you are not doing well, I think that choice can have implications for how well you are going to stay focused and put your attention on something to prevent distraction."

Again science and ancient wisdoms agree.

Initiating action and blocking out information play a large role in attention research. Diefendorff explained: "They are really two different self-regulating skills. One is the ability to chase a chosen activity and start it." And the other is to impair.

And of course this implies making sure that what you are about to activate is appropriate and right. In the light of self-regulation, Colonel Nally's warrior anthem comes to mind and can be a keen way to help focus on what you'll be needing to put your attention on when the time arises—even if only in general terms, it still turns on the right brain circuits for inhibition and activation: *Do the right thing, for the right reason, in the right way, with the brilliance of basics, even under extreme conditions.*

What this boils down to, for Diefendorff, is being able to devote your cognitive resources to the task du jour, so to speak, and have the motivation to initiate the activity.

Diefendorff's academic passions then surfaced and his voice intensified: "Initiative is critical," he said. "Once you've initiated an activity, you have to subsequently prevent distractions while you are pursuing that goal because we are living in a multi-goal environment where things are constantly vying for our cognitive resources, and some of us are really good [he says again with emphasis] at staying focused on something. Some of us aren't." And some of this ability, according to Diefendorff, can be acquired through practice and a lifetime of dealing with distraction.

So, there it was again: big as a neon sign, the way of change and mastery that is imbedded deep in our tissues, philosophies, and science. You can believe whichever argument makes the most sense for you, but the message is the same: train, practice, repeat, build a pattern, and acquire.

But remember: Be careful what you train because you are likely to attain it. I tell all of my students to keep their eyes open for any patterns that may emerge in their behaviors. Patterns suggest that something is being trained, consciously or unconsciously, and whatever that something is will eventually become automatic; you will then do it without thinking. Regulate what you train. And train the right things.

To this end, training, to me, has always involved mindfulness and willpower. So I asked Diefendorff if he could tell me more about what role these play for him in terms of activating goals.

He thought for a moment. "Yeah," he said. "I think that's what happens. At any given point in time, we have probably an infinite number of potential goals that are waiting for their opportunity, right? And I think that a really effective self-regulatory strategy is to wait for those opportunities to present themselves in the environment, then recognize them, and then initiate action at the appropriate time—not too late or too early—and that will facilitate the goal of trying to direct all your cognitive resources at that path."

One of the focuses of this book is on building behavioral procedures that can fire in milliseconds and help you toward a wide variety of goals. In terms of self-regulation, however, most researchers agree that one's inability to take control of the vast majority of automatic procedures is not a bad thing. Again, this condition exists because we rely on automatic functions. Some of these procedures, however, may get in our way as we attempt to pursue tasks, be they social, professional, academic, health-related, or what have you. Some may get in the way because we have changed our approach to doing certain things or because we have changed our perception of who we are and want to be. As a result, these procedures are ones we may want to take a close look at and perhaps rebuild, or short-circuit with procedures that are closer in line with our current life goals.

Diefendorff agrees. "It reminds me of something called *implementation intention*," he explained, "which says that a really effective way to pursue an activity is to specify when, where, why, and how you are going to pursue it, so that when you face the situation, you automatically turn your attention toward it. You essentially pass behavioral control from yourself to the environment and that allows you to not have to worry about the things you need to do. That in turn means you are more focused on what you are doing currently, and it also means you are pretty effective at starting things at the most opportune time."

Again science and ancient wisdom agree.

Diefendorff gave me a good example: "A person might think [visualize], 'When it's 4 o'clock I will leave work and pick up my son.' Or 'When I see Joe, I will initiate a conversation with him about a proposal I am working on.' So you're not having to worry about picking up your boy, you're not having to worry about finding Joe; you're not devoting your attentional resources to those goals. But when the situation is encountered, you've automatically and effectively initiated the action that's related to that goal."

Not so difficult, really. Remember the example of the yellow T-shirt at the goth concert? A coffeehouse friend of mine once told me about his son, who, at a very young age, was lying in bed one morning looking as if he was deep in thought. Seeing this, my friend asked, "So what are you thinking about so early in the morning?" "I'm just going over the things I want to do today," reported the son. Now add in the concept of visualizing your options and seeing which is best for you when opportunity knocks, and you have it. It's that simple, and in most cases you've already begun activating your potentialities as well as inhibiting distracters. In fact, I recently had Isabella, my daughter, try out the procedure to help her remember her placement on stage during a recent performance of *The Nutcracker*, and she was delighted with the results. Not difficult at all.

And so using your executive attention to help you activate or inhibit, in a selective, discriminatory way, things in your environment, you can integrate information stored in your memory (emotional, chemical, and procedural), and generate automatic actions with which you can pursue your goals, as well as free up brainspace for other things.

Diefendorff throws one more thing out for consideration: "The hallmark of effective self-regulation," he argues, "is perhaps not having one strategy or one set of strategies. It's about flexibility;

it's about being able to completely inhibit things you are not working on or at other times allowing yourself to be distracted by things because something may emerge in your environment as important. Someone who has only created inhibition may have missed an opportunity, right?"

The idea is to be fluid and adapt; what must be inhibited here may need to be activated there. The answer ultimately grows out of the circumstance.

Being flexible, according to Diefendorff, also means "You have to be able to persist with things until they're complete, and at the same time be able to prematurely disengage if the situation demands it, and I think that having an understanding at the executive level, so to speak, that what you're facing requires a certain amount of flexibility or not, is going to help individuals adapt or choose self-regulatory strategies that match the demand or hallmark."

We may be inclined to think that having great inhibition is always best. But Diefendorff insists that's not always true. Allowing yourself to be distracted because important things may come up is essential too. On a personal note, I have only to recall my colleague whom I let distract me smack in the middle of a research deadline and all of the benefits that I gained because of that decision. Or when I could have let the nurse explaining my EKG results (which turned out to be nothing) distract my fears. Or how Isabella's beautifully distracting dance that early morning in the kitchen brought my attention and attention research into a thrilling new journey.

James Diefendorff's research, for me, refines attention training into daily exercise. He shines a light into a circuitry capable of replacing the frailty of many hopes with vision and self-regulation—a brain-space where personal goals can become your reality.

Regulating This Way or That?

Consider this: You are reading about weather conditions in places such as Hawaii or the Bahamas, and then later you make a less favorable assessment of weather in a Midwestern city such as Indianapolis than you might have otherwise, completely unaware of how the first wave of information affected the other. Or you see a group of very attractive people; say, similar to runway models or handsome actors or actresses, and later judge a group of average-looking people as less attractive than you would have if you had not seen the more handsome people earlier. Or you look at an attractive Hollywood actress on the cover of a popular magazine and later have a less favorable view of yourself when you look in the mirror.

Then again, after reading about weather conditions in vacation places, your opinion about how satisfied people in those locations might be with their jobs may suddenly become more favorable than it would have been without having read about those places first.

The influence of informational biases has been well documented by psychologists. We are constantly assessing people, places, and things—as well as ourselves—often so quickly it happens unconsciously. Making judgments is part of life, but making attentive, accurate judgments may at times be delicate. This is because our perceptions can be contaminated by a large number of factors that gain access to our attention. For example, research shows that your emotional state prior to an assessment may have some influence on whether you react positively or negatively to certain information. Or that information preceding an assessment can prime your thoughts and actions, without your knowing it.

However, there are times when you become aware of such biases. To this end, researchers have found that when you become aware of biases, you tend to correct away from whatever information you perceive as false. But, similar research shows that you may actually associate with such information if you believe it has been told to you in confidence. If, for example, you think you are being told something false about a friend, you may respond contrarily to that information. Then again, say a friend tells you something about a coworker, and you believe you are being told this confidentially; you may then lean toward associating with what you are hearing. Either of these scenarios is capable of guiding your attention and subsequently your actions. What's more, the intensity of your responses can be affected by how much personal responsibility you perceive within the situation. Research additionally shows that the more responsible you believe you are for a judgment, especially when you perceive the judgment itself as important, and if you are not distracted, the more you tend to correct *away* from what you see as prejudicial information on the subject. The operative words here are *perceive* and *more.*

Yale psychologist Dr. Duane T. Wegener has reported extensive research on the way people correct for perceived bias. In a study conducted with Dr. Richard E. Petty of Ohio State University, Wegener explains that people tend to correct for perceived biases even when the actual bias is negligible. Furthermore, when you are motivated and can correct an assessment, in light of biased information, you tend to adjust your judgment in a direction opposite to that of the perceived prejudice.[7] This last point is important because your correction process will be the same even if your perceived bias is very different from the actual intensity of bias within a situation. For example, say you are on a hiring committee and someone points out that you have been steadily hiring only attractive applicants, and now it is time to hire for another position. Your perception of this as biased behavior, and its magnitude, can determine the intensity of your correction. The problem is that you may try to compensate for this pattern of hiring attractive people that has been brought to your attention. And you could, in the end, overcorrect to the extent to which you forge ahead and hire an "unattractive" person who is unqualified for the position. In contrast, you may see the person who is attempting to call your hiring criteria into question as attempting to bias you, in which case you may correct away from that information—that is, move in a direction opposite to what the person is suggesting. And then there is the scenario of not being consciously aware of the bias of certain information coming your way, in which case you tend to default and sway toward it.

Christian Wheeler's business objects research (from Chapter 3) provides another good example. In Wheeler's experiment, the briefcase increased the concept of competitiveness. So people were more ready to think about competitiveness in certain situations as well as see competitiveness in certain environments. However, "The fact that people were unaware in our studies," Wheeler explained, "doesn't mean that they would necessarily have to be unaware. For example, if you were to warn them before they came into the room that the objects in the room might influence their judgments, they may become attuned to those objects and try to eliminate their influence on their judgments."

Although it is not easy to decontaminate your attention from potential biases, there has been a lot of research on self-regulating bias correction that suggests there are a number of steps that can be taken for you to succeed.

Wheeler adds: Your first step would need to be identifying a source of bias. In the business objects experiment, for example, you had a briefcase and a pen. But, in your everyday experiences, sources could be any person, place, or thing you perceive as biasing your actions. The next step is to have some theory about the extent and the direction of bias, and how much. Then you have to decide how much to correct.

This again brings us back to the importance of executive attentional control and self-awareness, the combination of which enables you to not only make purposeful, discriminatory decisions, but to make them in line with who you have been, who you are presently, and who you want to be in the future.

Don't Forget the Other Guy

"B.F. Skinner had been one of my professors at Harvard," Dr. Pfaff told me when I asked about his thoughts on self-regulation. "So of course," said Pfaff genially, "behavior modification is the name of the game." Then he followed up with something that I have thought of many times since: "We [all of us] sometimes have a hard time knowing how to pay attention to things that are intrinsic." He paused as if carefully thinking about what he was about to say next. "In other words," he continued, "all of us, no matter how intelligent we are, will go barreling forth in life doing things mindless—and I use the word sort of in a Zen sense—mindless [he emphasized] to the underlying requirements of behavior in that epoch, at that place."

For me, the conversation had blossomed into an incredibly human moment, what Virginia Woolf would have called "a moment of being." Pfaff's humble observation, particularly as coming from a brain scientist so admired by so many, just put me in awe. I became humbled by his humility and have tried ever since to engender more of my own. I understood the kind of barreling he mentioned. Suffice to say, I've been there and done that.

Pfaff (both in his book, *Fair Play*, as well as in conversation) argued that the human brain is indeed hardwired for the capacity of mindful living. It seems, then, that the ability to reestablish a keen sense of attentive living is somewhere within our grasp.

Again, it all boils down to self-regulation. If you are content with the way you are presently attending to things, then regulation, for you, means that you keep going with that. If your life is demanding sharper attention or faster processing of information and you wish to establish that, then you can begin training your attention to that end. There are many possibilities, but the point is that perhaps there is more control within our grasp than we might have realized.

"I really have a lot of faith," Pfaff said, "in the malleability and improvement of human behavior." To Pfaff, self-regulation is a sort of sensitivity training. "So if you had a person," he says, "especially a child, who is having trouble relating to others and behaving in a civil fashion, a kind of caring fashion with other members of the group, I think it would be trying to ramp that person down to a level of quietude in which the person could be sensitive to the processes that allow that person's self image to become merged with or blurred with the other individual's image and thus behave in a better fashion."

According to Pfaff, our brains are wired for empathy. But he says rather matter-of-factly that although we may be wired for reciprocity, there are going to be individual differences, and there are going to be some people such as axe murderers who don't quite have the same capacity for these functions.

And so, of course, that again brings us back to the issue of attention training, and self-regulation, which begins with listening to ourselves (inside and out), as well as to others.

As Pfaff has been trained to see things physiologically, my training drives me to see metaphorically. I paused for a moment and considered the whole of our conversation. The educator in me wanted so much to put my finger on the heartbeat of Pfaff's theory—on its practical application to the world of attention research.

"I could make a metaphor of understanding empathy," I chuckled.

"What would that be?" asked Pfaff.

"I would liken it to biofeedback," I said.

Pfaff agreed. "Yes, yes," he said. "I think that's legitimate."

I remembered my sensei's words, "Stop thinking and pay attention." So much of paying attention, as my sensei suggested long ago, has to do with being motivated enough to just look at and listen to the sea of information that is your life and to then make predictions about where what you think, feel, and do might take you, and then simply opting for your best direction and then choosing accordingly.

Feedback, I thought—biochemical, emotional, electrical, sensory—it's all about feedback and mindfulness and intervention. It's all about attending to the "content" that is your mind, that is you. Choice, I thought, based on vision and predictability; the power to break away from conditioning, the power to be who you ultimately want to be. The power to be your self.

Before ending our conversation, I asked Pfaff one last question.

"So," I asked, "if you want to rebuild a behavior, mindful reflection would be a good place to start, yes?"

There was a moment of silence as I waited for an answer from this great thinker who has studied the brain and behavior for more than 30 years and who has been inarguably one of the most influential scientists of our time. Here at the end of my own journey I was looking for one more light, one more nod to help connect what has emerged in the pages of this book as a direct link beaming across millennia from the ancient world of holistic arts into the synaptic cellular conversations of frontier brain science.

"Yes," he said. "The notion of reflection and mindfulness is legitimate."

BEYOND OLD BELIEFS

*When one eye is fixed upon your destination, there is
only one eye left with which to find the way.*
—Anonymous

Some Landmarks in Attention Research

As far back as 1890, William James, perhaps the best known
of the early psychologists, talked of attention as an internal, mental process that keeps you alert and helps you clarify specific information or groups of information. Focus, to James, was an attentional
mechanism that could widen or narrow upon need. In his famous
text, *Principles of Psychology*, James argued that attention is essential to judgment, character, and will.[1]

Historically, these same concepts have also been core elements
of martial and other meditative arts training for more than 3,000
years. In this regard, one may think that not a lot has changed,
especially in terms of understanding human attention. What has
changed in our understanding, however, is the direction of attention research and how that might affect us. Let's take a look.

In 1929, Hans Berger invented electroencephalography or
EEG. Using the EEG, he was the first to describe different waves
appearing in the brain.[2] Today, EEGs are used in diagnosing a

variety of neurological conditions and disorders and have become significant in attention research, especially in providing a variety of options for treatment as well as self-regulation.

In 1935, John Ridley Stroop published an idea that became known as the Stroop Effect. Ever since, the discovery has been one of the most intriguing studies in psychology. Stroop noted that people's reactions were slower and that they made more errors when asked to identify words printed in colors differing from the word's actual meaning; for example, the word *yellow* appearing in red ink.[3] What was significant about Stroop's discovery was that he showed how information that is irrelevant to a specific task can in effect have a major impact on performance, leading to the success or failure of that task.

In 1946, the first successful nuclear magnetic resonance (NMR) was made.[4] These experiments eventually led to the 1977 discovery of magnetic resonance imaging (MRI) by Dr. Raymond V. Damadian, a professor at the State University of New York, Brooklyn.[5] Scientists insist the MRI has been all-important in identifying where certain attentional circuits are located in the brain, as well as how and when they fire.

In 1953, psychologist Colin Cherry discovered what he called The Cocktail Party Effect.[6] This effect, as mentioned earlier (see Chapter 1), demonstrates the ability to focus your listening on a single person among a roomful of conversations and to pay attention to selective information.

In 1958, English psychologist Donald E. Broadbent hit all attentional scopes with his publication of *Perception and Communication*, which took the world of information processing deeper into the realms of "unobservable mental processing."[7] Broadbent significantly advanced attention research to include more emphasis on information processing and the functions of selective attention.

Broadbent and Cherry essentially shifted traditional thinking of the mind as a sort of switchboard being triggered by information, to thinking of it as an information processor capable of its own selectivity and executive decision-making. And of course this movement in discovery was all fodder for future research into the possibilities of self-regulation.

Exploring the idea of information processing even further, psychologist Anne Treisman, an icon in the world of cognitive psychology and attention research and James S. McDonnell Distinguished University Professor of Psychology at Princeton University, published her theory of Feature Integration, which also argued and refined the perspective of information processing. In 1980, she "demonstrated, using the process of visual target search, that early vision encodes simple features in separate 'feature maps' and that focal spatial attention integrates them into a unified perception."[8] University of Louisville psychologist Wood Petry provides a great example of Treisman's theory: "Her theory explains why we see a red sports car driving by instead of an assortment of different features such as the color red, a shape in motion, and so on."[9]

Treisman's work continues to break new ground in the nature and limits of human perception, information processing, and priming—blazing the path forward for a plethora of attention research to come.[10]

Currently, as the majority of information shared in this book has suggested, emphasis in attention research has moved in the direction of how and why our attentional mechanism works as it does, what else can be done with it, and why at times our attentional mechanism fails. There has additionally been a burgeoning interest in how attention can be strengthened through self-regulation, particularly in areas of self-awareness, emotional control, motivation, and goal-setting.

A major finding within my own journey has been that there is not just one kind of attention. So it isn't fair to say that you either

have good attention or you don't, or that your attention is in deficit or not.

Indeed, as we move from one daily task to another we are all
momentarily deficient in some way. Overwhelming amounts of
research suggest that there are simply too many variables, and no
one attentional component you can simply switch on and say *there,
that's good attention*, or flip it off and say *there, that's not*.

Another major find within this book is that things can creep
into your attentional field without your knowing, and these items
can have great affect on what you think, feel, and how you act. To
be sure, they can hijack your attention, so to speak, at speeds so
unimaginably fast that we may believe we are calling our own
shots, as demonstrated in Wheeler's fascinating business-objects
experiment, even when we are told, in fact, that something else
may be influencing us. And so the question is, what do we do
against this?

A vast amount of current research, however, suggests that we
can have some say about what and how we attend. In this regard,
I am most intrigued by explorations in the realms of self-regulation.
At the end of the day, I believe that your ability to self-regulate is
what makes you free to be the real you, and me to be the real me.
Without the capacity to self-regulate, in a sense, the moment we
are in (the way we experience it, our potential for success, the pleasure we derive)—all these are in a guidance system in which we have
little or no influence. And this guidance system can orchestrate
everything from your thoughts, feelings, health, and relationships, to really all your daily endeavors.

To be aware in this world is to be like a child set free in a
universe of opportunity. As such, the act of conscious choice is
essential. Out of the millions of data competing for your attention
within every second of life, you have the power to choose. And at
that very moment, something within the world of consciousness
merges with something within the world of flesh and bone and
comes to life.

For the Future

There is significant need for more unbiased research in the area of ADHD and for the reporting of research that does not affirm the viewpoint that stimulants are an effective way of treating deficits in attention. It is becoming a well-known fact, for example, that an overwhelming amount of funding for ADHD research comes from the biopharmaceutical industry itself. A further complication is that many sponsors can wind up owning the data reported within these studies. The point is that stimulant drugs that are being prescribed for ADHD patients are strong medicine. It is important to remember that stimulants are controlled substances, are regulated by the DEA (drug enforcement agency), and thus require a narcotics license to prescribe. Thus, because ADHD is one of the most commonly diagnosed behavioral disorders in children, it is no surprise that there has been much concern regarding the use of these drugs—as well as toward the diagnosis itself.

ADHD, according to the American Psychological Association (APA) is characterized by persistent and developmentally inappropriate levels of inattention, impulsivity, and hyperactivity. However, there is good scientific evidence out there insisting that it may be a mistake to interpret these symptoms as conclusive of ADHD and as requiring treatment with stimulant medication. And this is of concern.

Dr. Lydia Furman, an MD and associate professor of pediatrics at Rainbow Babies and Children's Hospital in Cleveland, is passionate about the future of ADHD in terms of diagnosis, treatment, and research. When we spoke, she shared a variety of cautions regarding the accuracy of ADHD diagnoses as well as concerns about the stimulant drugs often used in its treatment.

"Yes, there are symptoms," she explained, "hyperactivity, inattention, and impulsivity—very important symptoms."[11]

Furman made it clear from the onset that she is not saying such problems don't exist or that they are not significant. My impression of her is that she likes to think things through completely before she speaks. Then she presents her views diligently and compassionately. Her voice is gentle and warm, and her philanthropy inspirational. She is easy to admire.

"In some cases," she said, "a child may be normal and yet there is a lack of tolerance and support from that child's environment. But clearly," she emphasized, "there are children who are beyond what would be expected for their age, with those particular problems. I guess where I break off from the rest of the pack is that I don't agree that that [list of symptoms only] makes a disease."

The operative word here is *disease*. Furman referred to the inadequacy of ADHD checklists. If you have never seen these, you can Google various examples pretty expeditiously and go through one yourself. The irony is strong. The series of "problems" alluded to in such checklists could be applied somewhat interchangeably to many of the highest—as well as the poorest—achieving students I have taught throughout the years, but what really stands out for me is that some of the most gifted students ever to walk through my classes could have perhaps been diagnosed with ADHD based on the criteria in these questionnaires.

The problem is, as Furman pointed out, "there are children who could meet the criteria for this "disease" who actually have a very important and needing-to-be-treated condition that would have been completely ignored if they had been placed on stimulant medications." This was an eye-opener for me. Most people with whom I discuss issues of attention deficit put their concern on whether an individual has it or not. But Furman sends another thought flashing into the mix. That is: There may in fact be something else of importance going on with many individuals diagnosed with ADHD—and *that* is going untreated. For example, she explained, "Children who have a serious learning problem, or children who have cognitive limitations, sometimes children who are gifted, children who have been abused—there are a lot of reasons a child might look that way. But if you don't, for instance, treat their educational problem, if you don't attend to their anxiety, if you don't remove them from an unsafe environment, yes they might look better—briefly—on medication, but you are not doing a service to that child."

These were strong thoughts. They made me consider all of the lost potential that could result from misdiagnosis—and again, what if the child is gifted? What happens to such gifts when they go unrecognized, un-nurtured, unrewarded? I wondered, is the destiny of such gifts to morph downward into problems? And if so, what a shame. What of emotional or social disturbances or unmet educational needs? What happens when these take seed, when weeks pass into months and months become years? These were tough questions, I thought, and should make us a lot more cautious with regard to drug treatment of ADHD.

Mounds of research and literature echo these apprehensions. In 1999, the National Institute for Mental Health (NIMH) published an impressive three-year study titled Multimodal Treatment Study for Children With ADD. What's very interesting is that the study was government funded for the purpose of looking at the effect of stimulant medication on children who are diagnosed with ADHD. The study used four groups of children; one group got meds, one got meds plus intervention in the form of a behavioral program, one got intervention in the form of community care, and one got just the behavioral treatment. At 14 months, of those four groups the medicated kids looked best. Then they went into what is called naturalistic subgroups—in other words, the trial no longer controlled what treatment they would receive. **And by the end of three years, results showed that receiving stimulant medication was a marker for behavioral deterioration.**

Commenting on the finding, Furman explained that "It wasn't due to a variety of things one would expect, like whether the children were on or off the medication—a variety of things in which you might say 'well that explains it.'" She thought for a moment, then continued. "I think it's an important trial and has not been discussed much in the media because it does not affirm the viewpoint that stimulants are an effective way of treatment. So I think there's scientific evidence out there that's concerning about [ADHD] treatment that's being given, but it hasn't been publicized very much."

After speaking with Dr. Furman, I spent a good amount of time reviewing more literature on the non-medicinal treatment of ADHD, and I did find a considerable amount, but, as she had suggested, it was not very well publicized.

Of interest, however, was research conducted by Dr. Rosemary Tannock, an associate professor of psychiatry at University of Ontario, who reports that ADHD symptoms show a marked overlap with other disorders as well as with reading disabilities and other communication/language disorders.[12] Tannock is a senior scientist in the Brain and Behavior Research Program at the Research Institute at the Hospital for Sick Children, in Toronto. She has additionally found in further studies that anxiety can interfere with the effective use of stimulants for children.

The problem with such overlaps, Furman notes, is that they can make it difficult to distinguish a child with inattentiveness due to emotional or psychological causes from one with a reading/language disability or other educational problem.

As such, Furman argues that "stimulant medications are extremely unlikely to be able to be of long-term and sometimes even short-term help to a child because they don't address the cause of the child's symptoms."

It is well documented that attentional problems can result from social or emotional experiences as well as other factors. Imagine a young boy walking home from school, say, who is ganged-up on by a half-dozen other boys who bully him and steal his new X-Box. Back in class, his attention is going to be everywhere except on his schoolwork, leaping around like what a psychologist once described to me as "spit on a griddle," and understandably so. The young boy, now hyper-vigilant because he was bullied, feels the flash of fear streaming along the low road through his amygdala, setting off fight-or-flight distresses that guide his attention away from his work. Time passes and he misses sequential lessons, resulting in a lack of understanding of concepts on which other concepts are built. He becomes lost. Soon the whole experience has a snowballing effect. In the end, and all too often, such a child is recommended to a pediatrician accompanied by complaints that he doesn't pay attention very well or that his mind is always wandering or that he can't focus for very long or that he's become a behavioral problem, and then comes the call for medication.

For Lydia Furman, however, internal and external stressors can have a lot to do with guiding attention. She emphasizes, "I think that the one message that I would like to convey is that a child who has symptoms of inattention, hyperactivity-impulsivity, needs an evaluation."

Why? Because there are too many possible variables affecting inattentiveness—an idea that has been at the heart of this book—regardless of whether you are talking about ADHD diagnosis or general inattentiveness. And so, central to effective attention treatment and/or training is one's understanding of where, when, how, and why things can go wrong as well as right with our attentional mechanism.

"These children need an educational evaluation *and* a psychological evaluation," Furman insists. "And, to me, stimulant treatment is essentially irrelevant."

I asked her to comment on her hope for the future. Without losing a beat, as if she had considered this question many times before, she added, "I would hope that instead of forging ahead with blinders on trying to create a biologic and genetic and neurologic basis for ADHD, I would hope that there could be a couple more people who would put the brakes on and say, let's look at the bigger picture. Let's try to look at this kid by kid. Let's try to look at what emotional, personal, developmental factors are involved for each child. So I guess stop driving the car forward. Stop, get out, and look at it."

Enter attention research icon Dr. Michael Posner, whose weave of cognitive, emotional, physical, and behavioral development, for children and adults, offers a wide variety of alternatives to stimulant treatment for inattentiveness. Studies conducted by Dr. Leanne Tamm (assistant professor of psychiatry at Southern Medical Center, Austin), Posner, and colleagues have shown significant improvements in attention via the use of specifically designed attention training materials, especially for the improvement of executive attention control.

Posner's training design places a lot of emphasis on self-regulation, particularly in areas of anticipation/prediction and selection of response choices. He then advances participants into more complex areas of memory and dealing with conflicting information by blocking irrelevant information. Tamm's reports that "Implementing attention training (ATT) with children at risk for attention and behavior problems may prevent or arrest impairments of attention."[13] As such, this kind of attention training is viewed as helpful to normal children as well as to those who experience a variety of developmental disorders that influence self-regulation.

A substantial amount of literature has been devoted to identifying and discussing such programs. For Tamm, Posner, and colleagues, the range of non-medicinal interventions seems wide. It includes activities from computerized game-like tasks, to video games, and even psychosocial initiatives such as parent groups in which parents learn how to utilize early intervention and prevention techniques for preschoolers with behavioral and attention problems. Most of these curriculums include parenting strategies that (in part) praise and attend, reward, and utilize when-then statements, problem-solving strategies, and a plethora of other skills intended to help the child gain more and better control.[14]

Posner insists that his brand of attention training has been successful in improving attention in normal adults and ADHD children. "Executive attention and effortful control [attention, focus shifting, inhibitory control] are critical for success in school," notes Posner. Considering whether they will someday be taught in pre-school, he says, "It sounds reasonable to believe so, to make sure all kids are ready to learn. Of course," he cautions, "additional studies will be needed to determine how and when."[15]

Although the world of brain science has made some spectacular discoveries in recent years, there will, of course, be more to come. At times, as may be the case with ADHD, some of the amazing technological advancements have thus far proven more illustrious than the actual amount of clarity they have been able to give in fully explaining issues such as ADHD. But it is my belief that technology and inquiry will together result in many new breakthroughs in attention research.

More research will be needed in the area of self-regulation, particularly in areas of interest, motivation, information processing, and priming as touched upon in this book. Research already suggests that self-regulating your attentional chain of command can be more powerful than any medication or underlying diagnoses in terms of whether attention is paid or not. Indeed, self-regulation may bridge the worlds of behavior modification with those of cognitive psychology, neurology, and biology—a process, I am happy to report, that has been the bedrock of most ancient holistic arts since their inception.

I am a firm believer that the more you understand about what goes on in your own head as you move from one moment of life to the next, the more purposeful, authentic, and happy a life you will create. Whichever language speaks loudest to you—that of science, that of arts, or both combined (my choice)—it is my hope that you will find deep, rich, and satisfying paths of living as a result. May the concepts shared in this book serve you well.

A Final Word

The exciting field of attention research has grown dramatically from the 1890s to the current day. Research trends suggest there is great potential for many more thrilling discoveries to be made in the years ahead. Such breakthroughs in theory are best left to the professionals, but the opportunity to benefit from such discoveries is best left to anyone and everyone interested.

Thanks to the abundance of research in the fields of psychology, neurology, neurofeedback, biology, and medicine, as well as in ancient arts that have withstood the test of millennia, a highly practical understanding of what attention is—its capabilities and trainability—has already been established and will light our way into the future.

Perhaps one of the most important understandings to have arisen from all this research is this: We can, with good certainty, actively choose to participant in how we attend to what matters in our lives and how this will contribute to the well-being of everything we touch. This is important because it gives us a say (and responsibility) in our destiny and in that of others. It helps us make the most of our present, paint our future with aspiration, and edit our past.

A student of mine recently told me that she had done something in one of her college classes that she believed would ruin her relationship with the professor for the rest of the semester. Along this same line, a friend commented, after finding out that I had been writing a book involving the likes of stem cell research, neurology, and psychology, "You're not going to start telling us that we are hopelessly doomed are you?" She expressed this based on her fear that science was going to tell her that we are all simply slaves to a preset pattern of chemicals and electrical sparks.

"Just the opposite," I said. "My message is that you, we, each of us have a choice." One of the most important finds of this book, in fact, has been that we are all literally wired to participate in what happens to us. If my student, for instance, chooses not to attend to what occurred with her professor, then yes, having her problem extend throughout the entire semester is really a possibility. But she could reflect on ways to edit whatever procedure(s) went wrong in her rapport with her teacher, short circuit it so that it doesn't occur again, and thoughtfully come up with a new procedure capable of triggering a different response from her teacher (in a way that can be perceived as unbiased). She can have a say in how the rest of her semester goes—if she chooses.

My journey into human attention has left me more convinced than ever that we can establish a lot more ownership of and direction for our lives. So my next message is to be mindful. And I'm not going to say that this is easy. Mindfulness is work. But it can give you the control you seek, rather than abandoning your destiny to the mass of circuits and chemicals that are as much a part of your reality as your deepest desires.

Accordingly, there is no doubt that some of the most exciting research ahead will be in the areas of self-regulation. Because, in the end, isn't this what it's all about—seeing and understanding your deepest self, becoming the person you were born to be, feeling free and confident and happy?

I have always believed that one of the greatest gifts you can return to the world in exchange for consciousness is the fully developed voice of your own unique awareness—the gift of your self. *Can I Have Your Attention?* began with the first flickers of such an idea fully alive in the spontaneous and uncontaminated dance of a little girl still in the opening nights of her life's performance. And no matter where this journey landed along the way, each step— one way or another—has come back to the notion of self. To my daughter, Isabella, life is indeed a stage, and she is both dancer and choreographer. And so are we all.

In this spirit, I have included as an Afterword to *Can I Have Your Attention?* a series of strategies you can use to help shape and improve your own attention, with the hope that you may discover newfound success in all aspects of everyday life.

AFTERWORD

A USER'S GUIDE TO HIGH-SPEED, ACCURATE ATTENTION

When mindfulness is achieved, the 'I' of a person is capable of watching what is happening in body, emotions, and mind without reacting. Instead, the 'I' acts in whatever way seems useful from its transpersonal point of view, which in Zen is called the point of view of the True Self.
—E. Green and K.S. Ozawkie

A Trip to the Mall

See how many attention concepts you can apply to the following scene: Picture yourself walking through a mall with your partner. He or she is talking and you are listening. At the same time, you are being inundated with millions of bits of information that want your attention. You can, at any time, select a few of these and disregard the rest. Neon signs bearing the names of stores flash arrays of colors across the midway, and merchandise in brightly lit storefronts reflects in the corner of your eye. Your brain's auditory center informs you of music playing in the background as you walk past a food court that your olfactory centers say have sweetened the air with everything from Japanese stir-fry to warm cinnamon buns. You see someone bite into a freshly baked pretzel and notice your own mouth watering as if you had just taken a bite yourself. Your partner asks you a question. Your thoughts suddenly narrow as you consider what you will say. You respond. Now your partner is talking again. You shift your attention to his or her voice and body language, which you perceive as saying that you answered the question satisfactorily. You notice that your partner's response to your answer makes you feel good inside.

As you continue walking, you pass through streams of people dressed in the most interesting of ways. Suddenly one of these people looks familiar. For a moment, you think it is someone from work. Your amygdala starts speaking in small shockwaves to let you know something's not right. It hits you that you really don't want to see this person on your time off. Your tension spikes. Your focus tightens and you check the person out more closely. *Whew*, you think, *just a case of mistaken identity*. In a few moments' time, the rush of adrenaline you felt disappears and you are feeling more calm. You ask your partner to repeat the last thing he or she said before you tensed up and gave so much attention to the person you thought you recognized that you faded out on what your partner was saying. Your partner backtracks and begins again. At the same time, your attention flows to a couple walking hand-in-hand. You catch part of their conversation and then abandon it for the scent of perfume on a nearby display, which momentarily sends your mind back a few years to someone you used to know, and all the while you're looking for the hallway that will lead you to a certain shop that will hopefully carry a product you would like to purchase.

You toggle back and forth from the conversation you are having with your partner to keeping your eye peeled for the store, which you know is in the vicinity of one of the candle shops—and, by the way, your olfactory centers are already sending you messages of vanilla- and lavender-scented candles so you know that you're getting close. You remember a logo above the front window of the candle shop. You see it. Once inside the shop you've been looking for, your focus narrows as you locate the aisle that will have the item you want to purchase. Your focus narrows even further as you look among various products. When you locate the one you want, you notice there are two versions, a generic one and a brand-name one. You pick them both up and begin reading labels. Your focus narrows even further. As you read, you experience a déjà vu—another time, another place—you were faced with a similar decision, of whether to buy generic or brand-name. You remember purchasing the generic product, to save a bit on cost, and then finding that you were not happy with the results. You also recall a friend who told you in confidence that he has used the same product and has always found the name brand to be better. You look at the labels again and in the end choose the name brand. Your focus widens again almost immediately as you automatically head for the cash register and pay.

In a way, this part of your trip could be described as on automatic pilot. You are suddenly opening your focus to its widest setting to take in as many sites and sounds as possible, while at the same time easily toggling in and out of conversation with your partner. You head out of the mall with this mindset, certain storefronts catching your attention as markers telling you turn right here, turn left there. When you get to the parking lot, a large blue truck parked at the end of a certain row of parking slots catches your eye. You suddenly know to turn down that row because that is where you have parked. You know that you are looking for a gray Honda. You don't think about it much until you believe you see a car of that make and color. Your focus suddenly narrows. But when you look for a specific sticker on the rear window, you notice it is not there. Wrong car, you conclude. You widen your focal gate again, and when you spot another gray Honda, you again look for the sticker, and this time it is there. *That's my car*, you think, and you are correct.

Attention researchers can examine each of the steps in this account of a simple shopping trip and break down much of what you are encountering psychologically, neurologically, and biologically. Indeed, modern neuroscience could provide images of various brain centers firing in milliseconds as competing data battle to win your attention and your focus moves from one thing to another. But the good news is that you don't have to have a PhD to begin to understand what is going on in your own head. With the right basic concepts, you too can begin to unravel some of the mysteries regarding your attention's inner workings.

By this point, you can probably identify many components of attention in the simple scenario we just played out as well as see the functional or dysfunctional contributions of each to the experience. Armed with these basics—and a variety of techniques for self-regulation—you should be able to make some real strides in training your attention. Let's take a look at a few of these techniques.

Stay Close to Center

Realistically you can focus on anything you wish, and as we have seen, you will hardly ever be short of details from which to choose.

Confucius maintained that in order to choose well, "You must stay close to center." Otherwise your actions, no matter how spectacular, run the risk of irrelevance, or worse, dysfunction. So in Eastern thought, centeredness precedes action.

As such, your first act of self-regulation is to put the sum of your cognitive resources on self. It doesn't matter whether you believe that within the perimeter of this special place is the deepest representation of your personality or whether it represents your purest source of consciousness or whether it is, indeed, the very seat of your soul. What's important is that you live as much as possible from this vortex, selecting what things in your environment you want to integrate with other forms of information you have stored in your memory (emotional, biochemical, and procedural) as you create the procedures that will help you achieve your life's goals.

Xin-Yi

There is another way you can think about center. In Chinese the term *Xin-Yi* means *heart-mind* and is a core concept in martial arts and consciousness training. Believed by the ancient masters to be enormously empowering, Xin-Yi is perhaps one of the most coveted mindsets you can attain. Here is how it works. By targeting your attention to Xin (heart consciousness), you feel—make yourself aware of—what is presently most important and natural for you. *Heart consciousness* refers to what is truly in your heart, not what other factors in your environment desire for you. So you have to be careful and through reflection take your time, peer into your deepest self, and get this right. Yi (intention) is the mind's power for directing energy—using your brain's reasoning power to aim you toward what you want. The idea of Xin-Yi is that when you finally make your move, you proceed from a place of heart-mind. Note this word is hyphenated, meaning unified, not separate as in heart *and* mind. With practice Xin-Yi becomes automatic.

Using Attention-Training Strategies

Each self-regulation strategy that is provided in this section is constructed for use as a regulatory intervention that can be used in a wide range of situations. Repetition is the hallmark of attention training. Repetition of any of these strategies or some of your own creations will integrate your conscious and automatic processing. Be flexible and creative in adapting strategies to fit your personal experiences. Once added to your long-term memory, you will be able to access them as procedures on a continuing basis. Allow for customizing any strategy to new goals. In the words of Dr. Deirdre V. Lovecky, director of the Gifted Resource Center of New England, researcher and author, "speed is not as important as getting there." Dr. Lovecky shared this thought with me back at the beginning of my journey into human attention. Her advice reminded me of something my sensei used to emphasize so many years ago: "What good is speed if you are doing things that are detrimental?" he would say. "Concentrate on getting your techniques right and train them. Speed will come later. But it will come." And always stay close to center.

Strategy for Self-Scanning

Try this quick and easy three-step scan next time you approach any goal. It can work before or even during daily tasks.

Step One. Focus all of your attention on your self. Then ask the following questions:

- **Where am I at the moment?** Identify your environment.

- **What do I want to gain from the situation?** Identify your goals in order of importance.

- **What should I gain from the situation?** Consider what you feel you should gain from the situation. Then examine whether this is different from your desires and how these work to modify your behaviors.

- **What have I done in similar situations in the past?** Identify your past actions.

- **Do I want to behave differently?** Identify any behaviors you don't want to repeat.

- **If so, how?** Identify how you can avoid these actions. Note: Any procedures you create here will, through repetition, become habit, and from there become automatic for future experiences.

Step Two. Consider your environment. Then ask the following questions:

- **What do others expect to gain from the situation?** Identify and prioritize these.

- **What attention does my environment demand from the situation?** For example, *I can only speak when it is my turn. I have to use professional language.*

- **What information should be activated?** For example, *It may be best if I am calm at this point of a lecture or meeting and if I don't ask questions.*

- **What information should be inhibited?** You can, for example, suppress frustrations and irrelevant information. For example, teachers, businesspeople, and the like may have to convey an emotion that is inconsistent with how they feel in order to reach their goal. A student may be highly motivated to do well in school, but if that person has poor inhibitory functioning, he or she may not reach the desired goal. If you are reflecting, ask, *What distracters can I anticipate and thus inhibit when they present themselves?*

Step Three. Look for a match. Examine whether the information you have collected is in synch with behaviors (feelings and actions) you are outputting. If they are well matched, then continue doing things as you are. If there is a mismatch, then adjust or correct accordingly. Note: With repetition, this entire strategy can become automatic, freeing up brain space as well as predictable worry and giving you more cognitive power to stay focused on other things.

Strategy for Correcting Perceived Biases

Remember that you tend to correct against perceived biases and to the extent that you perceive the intensity of a certain bias. However, also remember that you tend to sway toward prejudicial information when you do not perceive it as biased or when you see it as confidential.

You can try to correct for perceived biases by following this strategy:

- Imagine trying to correct your behavior around a certain person. Maybe there is something about this person that makes you really aggressive or angry and you don't want to do that anymore.

- Make yourself aware that this person has that influence on you.

- Make your goal of correction important and make yourself responsible for its outcome.

- Then, try to figure out how much influence he or she has on you.

- Finally, try to correct that much so that you're acting normal.

Note: These same steps can be used for anything that you think is influencing your behavior in a way you don't want. Try your best to adjust for the correct amount, keeping in mind that you may be incorrect. In fact, keeping your mind attuned to the possibility of error will help you in your assessment of new information coming at you as you work toward your goal.

Strategies for Listening to What Your Hormones Are Saying

This strategy asks that you focus on your body chemistry. You can do this on-the-fly by pausing and taking a quick inventory or through reflection or meditation. The idea is to put your attention on peripheral hormonal effects.

Strategy One. Synchronize your body chemistry with imminent goals. Focus all of your attention on your self. Then ask the following questions:

- Where am I at the moment?

- What do I want to gain from the situation?

- What should I gain from the situation?

- What hormones are speaking? What are they saying?

- How has this body chemistry affected me in similar situations in the past?

- Do I want to change how it affects me?
- If so, how?
- Is my body chemistry facilitating or hindering this change?
- If it is hindering, ask what you can do to compensate, and do it. If it facilitates, keep doing what you are doing.

Strategy Two. Attain mental calmness. Try the following activities to increase hormonal influence on mental calmness.

- Eat right and exercise. Low levels of serotonin and dopamine have been associated with depression, irritability, and lack of focus. Research shows that eating balanced meals with lots of protein, particularly that found in eggs, meats, and complex carbohydrates such as whole grains (breads, crackers, and the like) for snacks may help. Avoid simple carbohydrates such as cakes, pastas, white breads, and candy. Exercise can also be of great help in boosting these levels.
- Socialize. Increase your depth of friendship and social interaction.
- Increase intimacy. Partners can increase touch, massage, and sex. These are great for heightening levels of oxytocin, serotonin, and dopamine, as well as decreasing levels of stress-related hormones.

Strategy Three. Use a system of self-reward.

- Establish a self-reward system by increasing your sense of responsibility (but not overwhelmingly) for achieving certain goals so that when you achieve them you will feel a greater sense of accomplishment.
- Launch a series of smaller achievable goals en route to the bigger one. See the attainment of each smaller goal as a significant rung on the ladder toward achieving the largest one.

- Increase the value you place on certain goals by seeing the pleasure they can bring to you and others.

- Actively put yourself in an environment in which there are others who highly value the same goals as you and will see the significance of your accomplishments.

- Intentionally inhibit the influence of those who do not share these values. But use discretion. You don't want to close yourself off from something important.

Strategy Four. Be aware of cycles and patterns for calmness and stress.

Imagine trying to correct a behavior that you feel is influenced in a negative way by certain body chemistry. Then ask yourself the following questions:

- What people, places, and things bring forth the peripheral effects of this chemical reaction?

- To what intensity?

- When, where, and why does this influence occcur?

- How does feeling this way affect my ability to focus and my mood?

- What can I do to sway my response in the other direction? For example, you can sometimes compensate by changing the nature of your goal. This can be done in many different ways. Say, for example, you have accepted employment for a low-status position and your actions are negative as a result. You can try placing greater value on the position by seeing it as a smaller goal connected to larger goals (such as providing additional experience on your resume for other jobs you can seek within, say, a year or less). You could perhaps connect the job to funding more education that will, in turn, open up more exciting employment opportunities. Or you could see it as funding your ability to move to a more desirable location, which you see as opening new employment, educational, and/or social opportunities.

- What people, places, things, thoughts, and memories have the opposite effect?

- Ask yourself, *How can I activate these during predictable trouble spots to help balance things out?* For example, I had my daughter put a shiny sticker of her choice on my office key so that it is the first thing I see before entering in the morning. A little thing like that can prime me into a good mood. Repetition will help make all of these strategies automatic. Try this same process to ramp a variety of moods, such as calmness, quick bursts of energy, and so on.

Note: You can utilize your mirror system to help you see how some of these influences play out in your actions—in other words, generally those around you will mirror back what you put out. You can also use your ability to inhibit or activate predictable patterns by telling yourself, *When I see_____, I will do thusly* (take a deep breath and consider my options). Or, *When I see _____, I will mark it irrelevant*, thereby freeing up brainpower for other things you want to focus on and relying on higher speed automatic procedures to take care of business.

Strategies for Listening to Your Emotions

Strategy One. Matching your emotions to imminent goals and vice versa is an essential part of paying attention. There are two aspects to self-regulating your emotions; the first is self-awareness: understanding yourself, your goals, your intentions, and your responses/actions. The second aspect is empathy: your understanding of how others feel and your ability to accurately predict the consequences of your actions on them and then back to you. As such, impulse control, which is your ability to delay gratification, is critical to this kind of regulation.

Your first job is to look for the pattern of components that integrate and as a result trigger behavior in an otherwise seemingly unified occurrence. Note: Self-regulation adjusts the integration of such components to satisfy goals: *I feel anger, but that's okay because I like this person.* Or *This is unfair, therefore I will intervene.*

The following strategy will help you put your attention on the right emotional components to help you flow through goals of all kinds.

- What specific emotion am I feeling?
- What "cool" information am I receiving?
- Is there a disjunction? If so, why?
- Has my feeling this way negatively affected similar situations in the past?
- Has it ever affected similar situations in a positive way?
- Are there things I do better when I am operating under this emotional influence? If so, what?
- Are there things I do worse?
- What are my best options for action under the influence of what I am feeling?

Pick your best option and do it. Let yourself see the value and feel the reward of your accomplishment.

Strategy Two. Try this strategy if you are feeling caught in a downward spiral. Ask yourself:

- How have such spiraling moods affected me in similar situations in the past?
- What things are not facilitated? Tell yourself that things can and will change and not to invest so much in certain perspectives.
- What things are facilitated by these mood shifts?

Pick something you do well under the influence of mood shifts and do that. Again, let yourself see the value and feel the reward of your accomplishment.

Strategy Three. Try this strategy next time you feel that inflated emotions may be affecting your thoughts and actions as you approach a certain goal. Ask yourself:

- What positive emotions am I feeling?
- Are any of these emotions inflating my judgments? Which?
- How has feeling this way impacted similar situations in the past?
- How might feeling this way impact me now as I pursue this goal?

If what you are feeling facilitates, go with it. If not, ask, *How can I compensate?* Then adjust and move forward. Let yourself see the value and feel the reward of your accomplishment.

Strategy Four. Empathy is an important people skill related to your ability to listen to your emotions and put them in synch with specific goals. By putting your attention on doing unto others, so to speak, as you would have done to you, you deepen your emotional self-awareness as well as your ability to predict the consequences of your behaviors. Researchers have known for years that people who are more empathic are more successful at work and in their personal lives.

The following strategy is based on my conversation with Dr. Donald Pfaff and his theory that we are wired for altruism. Try it to help tap your brain's capacity for empathy. The next time you approach an important goal, ask yourself:

- What am I about to do? See the action/behavior in your mind.
- What is the target of my action, in terms of person, place, or thing?

- How will this action/behavior affect both your self and the target of the action? You can determine this by merging what you are about to do, the target of your action, and your self.

- Is this a good thing to do? If so, do it. If not, don't.

You can engage in this process either in the middle of things or in advance through visualization. You can also use reflection after certain experiences to help fine-tune procedures for the next time the situation arises. Let yourself see the value and feel the reward of your accomplishment.

Strategy for Prioritizing

You can prioritize things in advance. Remember, at any given moment you are inundated with enormous amounts of information. There is no way anyone can gain control of all of it—or even a lot of it. But you can inventory the big picture of your life and the specifics that make it up and pick and choose which elements you want to protect, activate, enhance, change, follow, improve, or eliminate. Results won't happen overnight. However, if you begin by regulating even one or two larger items per year and several smaller en route, leaving room for popup items that appear on a per diem basis, you will make a solid change in the overall big picture of your life fairly soon.

Identify an aspect of your life you would like to improve. Try the following strategy. Ask yourself:

- What do I want from this situation?

- What do others expect me to gain from it?

- What am I currently doing to work toward this goal?

- What, if anything, am I doing procedurally or feeling emotionally that impairs my progression toward this goal?

- What am I doing or feeling that facilitates my progression?

- What procedures, if any, do I need to create to help me eliminate old dysfunctional ones that have been getting in my way—at any link in the chain?

- What attributes do I have that can help me in pursuit of this goal?

- What skills will I need to acquire? Are they attainable? When, where, how, and how much time will I need?

- How much lasting power does this goal have?

- What other life-goals are affected by this goal—positively and negatively?

- What smaller goals can be linked into a chain of tasks to help me pursue my larger goal?

- What is the best chronological order to begin implementing them into my daily activities?

- Does it make sense to pursue this goal?

If so, prioritize and begin implementing.

Strategy for Re-Gating

Use your executive attention to properly gate situations. You may want to, at first, set this up via visualizations and reflections. These can then be automated through repetition. Only remember that you will want to allow yourself the opportunity to add further information in the future.

To help you gate your attention, consider these questions on-the-fly or preferably in advance, next time you approach a goal or task. Ask yourself:

- Where am I?
- What do I want to gain?
- What do others want to gain?
- What mutual information are we sharing, sensory and otherwise?
- What mutual information should we share, sensory and otherwise?
- What inputting information needs to be amped up?
- What needs to be impaired?
- In what similar situations have I been in the past?
- What has facilitated my focus?
- What has gotten in the way of my focus?
- What primes can I establish to short-circuit dysfunctions? For example, *When I enter the room and see my coworkers, I will remember to empty my mind of any negativity and begin speaking with the gentle amiability I exhibited my first day on the job.*
- What primes can I set up to activate things that facilitate? *When I see Leo, I will remember to listen at least as much as I speak.*

Experiment a lot and enjoy.

NOTES

Notes attributed to interviews are cited. Unless otherwise attributed, any further accounts that refer to these scientists are from those interviews.

Chapter 1

1. Dr. Tram Neill, interview conducted December 2007.

2. Neill, W.T. "Perception," 312–314.

3. Frank Vellutino, interview conducted December 2007.

4. Dr. Todd Wysocki, interview conducted January 2008.

5. There is a lot of literature on component models for attention. You may wish to see: (A) McKay Moore Sohlberg and Catherine A. Mateer, *Introduction to Cognitive Rehabilitation: Theory and Practice* (New York: Guilford Press, 1989). (B) Alvaro Fernandez, "Training Attention and Emotional Self-Regulation: An Interview with Michael Posner."

6. "Meditation May Fine-Tune Control Over Attention."

7. Ibid.

8. Warm, Joel, "Are You Really Paying Attention?" *This story and accompanying video were originally produced for the American Institute of Physics series Discoveries and Breakthroughs in Science by Ivanhoe Broadcast News.*

9. Dr. Fernando Miranda, interview conducted February 2008.

10. "Meditate To Concentrate." For more on Davidson's terrific work with meditation, see a story that appeared in the *Washington Post* at *www.washingtonpost.com/wp-dyn/articles/A43006-2005Jan2.html.*

11. Jackson, Maggie, *Distracted*, 256.

12. Sakai, Jill, "Meditation May Fine-Tune."

13. "Brain Scans Show Meditation Changes Minds, Increases Attention."

14. Cullen, Lisa Takeuchi, "How to Get Smarter, One Breath at a Time."

15. "Brain Scans Show Meditation Changes Minds, Increases Attention."

16. "Meditate To Concentrate."

17. Othmer, Siegfried, PhD, and Caroline Grierson, RN, "Biofeedback."

18. "Attention / IQ / Academic Performance."

19. "What is Neurofeedback?"

20. For a fuller view of neurofeedback, take a look at this terrific resource sponsored by The International Society for Neurofeedback and Research: *www.isnr.org.*

21. Colonel Kevin Nally, interview conducted December 2007.

22. Dr. Donald Ward, interview conducted December 2007 and December 2008.

Chapter 2

1. Dreifus, Claudia, "A Conversation With Joseph LeDoux.

2. Ibid.

3. "Runner's High Demonstrated."

4. Johnson, Steven, *Mind Wide Open*, 138.

5. Vedhara, K., and J. Hyde, et al., "Acute Stress."

6. Latham, Catherine, "Sharpbrains."

7. Lupien, Sonia, "Stress."

8. Amen, Daniel G. *Change Your Brain*, 81.

9. Kramer, Peter, *Listening to Prozac*, 89–100.

10. Dr. Stanley Glick, PhD, MD, interview conducted July 2008.

11. Marano, Hara Estroff, "Why We Dream."

12. Carver, Joseph M., PhD, "Dopamine."

13. Begley, Sharon, *Train Your Brain*, 248.

14. Carver, Joseph M., PhD., "Dopamine."

15. "Study Focuses on Progression of Menopause and Memory Loss."

16. Dr. Robert Josephs, interview conducted July 2008. Also read more about Josephs' and colleagues' study, "Testosterone, Cognition, and Social Status," at *http://homepage.psy.utexas.edu/homepage/faculty/josephs/pdf_documents/Test_Stat_Cog2005_H&B.pdf.*

17. Boyd, Kevin. "Testosterone Aids Older Men's Brains."

18. For more about Dr. Shelly Taylor's study, see Beth Azar's "Emotion Drives Attention: A New Stress Paradigm for Women." *Monitor on Psychology* 31, No. 7, July/August 2000.

Chapter 3

1. Claparede tells a complete version of this amazing story in: Rappaport, David, Ed., *Organization and Pathology of Thought*. New York: Columbia University Press, 1951, 58–75. (Original work published in 1911.)

2. LeDoux, Joseph, *The Emotional Brain*, 190.

3. "Emotion Drives Attention."

4. "IQ Test: Where Does it Come From?"

5. Goleman, Daniel, *Emotional Intelligence*, 4.

6. Ibid.

7. Ibid

8. Dr. John Mayer, interview conducted July 2008.

9. Goleman, Daniel, *Emotional Intelligence*, 45.

10. Ibid., 73.

11. Goleman, Daniel, "The Brain Manages Happiness and Sadness in Different Centers."

12. Johnson, Steven, *Mind Wide Open*, 58.

13. Schoenherr, Neil, "Flashbulb Memories."

14. Hyams, Joe, *Zen in the Martial Arts*, 48–49.

15. For a more complete explanation, see "A Mindful Self and Beyond: Sharing in the Ongoing Dialogue of Buddhism and Psychoanalysis" at *www.advaitacentrum.nl/04_Studiecentrum/ Psychotherapie/Pt_A_Waning2*.

16. Damasio, Antonio, *Descartes' Error*, 67–68.

17. Whiting, Wythe L., et al., "Overriding Age Differences," 223–232.

18. Dr. Wythe Whiting, interview conducted October 2008.

19. To view and read more, see "Top-Down Processing and Episodic Memory" in Vassar College's *Psychology in the News*, at *http:// intro2psych.wordpress.com/2007/11/25/top-down-processing-and-episodic-memory*.

20. Whiting, Wythe, L., et al., "Overriding Age Differences," 223–232.

21. Neill, W.T., "Perception," 312–314.

22. Nicholson, Christy, "Memory and Consciousness."

23. Gladwell, Malcolm, *Blink*, 256–259.

24. Dr. Christian Wheeler, interview conducted November 2008.

25. Dr. Donald Pfaff, interview conducted October 2008.

26. Pfaff, Donald, *The Neuroscience of Fair Play*, 66.

27. Hampson, Rick, "New York City Cheers Death-Defying Rescuer."

28. Pfaff, Donald, *The Neuroscience of Fair Play*, 202–203.

Chapter 4

1. Posner, Michael I., and Mary K. Rothbart, "Attention, Self-Regulation and Consciousness." You can also view online at *www.pubmedcentral.nih.gov/ picrender.fcgi?artid=1692414&blobtype=pdf*.

2. Lurie, A.R. *The Working Brain*.

3. Norman, D.A., and T. Schallice. "Attention to Action: Willed and Automatic Control of Behavior," in Posner, Michael I., and Mary K. Rothbart, "Attention."

4. Fernandez, Alvaro, "Training Attention."

5. Dr. James Diefendorff, interview conducted November 2008.

6. Diefendorff, James M. "Perceived Self-Regulation," 228–247.

7. You can see this very exciting and interesting study in full in: Wegner, Duane, "Flexible Correction Process in Social Judgment: The Role of Naive Theories in Corrections for Perceived Bias." *Journal of Personality and Social Psychology* 68, No. 1:36–50 (1995).

Chapter 5

1. "Classics in the History of Psychology."

2. "Hans Berger."

3. EPLab OnLine Measures, "Stroop Task."

4. "History of MRI."

5. Barker, Leslie, "Who Invented the MRI?"

6. "Cocktail Party Effect."

7. "Donald Eric Broadbent."

8. "Anne Treisman, PhD."

9. "Current Winner: 2009—Anne Treisman."

10. "How Do We Perceive Objects?"

11. Dr. Lydia Furman, MD, interview conducted December 2008.

12. Purvis, Karen L., and Rosemary Tannock, "Language Abilities in Children With Attention Deficit Hyperactivity Disorder."

13. Tamm, Leanne, PhD, et al. "Can Attention Itself Be Trained?"

14. Ibid.

15. Fernandez, Alvaro, "Training Attention."

GLOSSARY

adrenal glands: responsible for regulating stress, these star-shaped glands sit atop the kidneys. *Renal* indicates their association with the kidneys.

adrenaline rush: refers to an activated adrenal gland or fight-or-flight response.

alternating attention: the ability to toggle from one task to another and from one piece of incoming information to another.

anosognosics: individuals with damage to their emotional centers.

attention deficit: in general, refers to shortage of attention (specifically with regard to any one of attention's components), inattentiveness, and ADD/ADHD.

automated: robot-like. Processes and systems can be considered automated and can conserve other mental requirements, freeing them up for other tasks.

beginner's mind: attaining the plain and simple attention of an infant. The term is used in the study of Zen Buddhism and Japanese martial arts.

bottom-up processing: information processing guided by data input.

brainwaves: electrical activity produced by the brain and recorded by an electroencephalograph (EEG).

bushido: samurai moral code.

Cocktail Party Effect: the ability to focus your listening on a single person among a roomful of conversations and to pay attention to selective data.

cognitive: involving cognition or the processes of knowing through perception, learning, and reasoning.

corollary discharge: a mechanism in the brain that allows one to distinguish between self-generated and external stimuli or perceptions.

cortisol: steroid hormone triggered by mental or physical stress.

declarative knowledge: a distinction in knowledge made by philosopher Gilbert Ryle. In common language, the distinction is made most clearly when we say "know *that.*" Declarative knowledge is propositional (has a truth value).

declarative memory: memory that can be discussed; memory that stores facts, as opposed to procedural memory, which stores procedures or skills.

detachment: taking attentional inventory of your internal and external environments.

DNA: a double-stranded molecule that encodes genetic information.

dojo: the place where martial arts are learned and trained.

dopamine: euphoric brain drug associated with reward-seeking behaviors.

downward crash: downward-spiraling moods.

emotional congruency: the act of matching pieces of similar emotional information.

emotional intelligence: understanding your own feelings, as well as your empathy for the feelings of others, and the ability to regulate your own emotions such that they enhance living.

emotional memory: the brain's warehouse for emotional events.

empathy: your ability to feel what other people are feeling, which allows you to predict the consequences of your actions. As such, empathy provides you more information with which to gauge your responses as you work toward daily goals.

empty mind: also known as *mushin*, empty mind is a calming technique practiced by most martial artists. The point is to empty the mind of all assumptions and negative emotions.

encoding: helps you place things in storage as working memory.

endocannabinoid anandamide: a brain chemical similar to THC, the active chemical found in marijuana.

endocrine gland: a gland that secretes a hormone into the bloodstream.

endogenously: externally.

error management training: training employees how to perform a task, especially with regard to dealing with errors.

estrogen: steroid sex hormone commonly associated with women.

executive attention: attention's CEO, it has the split-second ability to override impulses and attractions for more favorable understated options.

exogenously: internally.

fatty acid: an important component of lipids (fats) in plants, animals, and microorganisms.

fear-based memory: emotional memory.

feature integration: a theory of information processing developed by Anne Treisman, suggesting that certain information, such as the basic features of an object, could be processed unconsciously as well as separately and then integrated.

fight-or-flight: primitive survival instinct, a response to threat.

flashbulb memory: associated with highly emotional, traumatic incidents.

focused attention: ability to focus on sensory data.

form: when used in this text to describe part of the mind, form refers to the actual cells that make up your brain.

gating: the act of adjusting how much sensory data you take in or out.

glucose: a simple (monosaccharide) sugar, as in honey.

glycogen: a polysaccharide and main source of energy; stored in the liver.

homeostasis: physiological equilibrium.

Homo sapiens: humans.

hot information: emotions.

hypnoidal: hypnotic.

kata: a term for martial arts techniques linked together and performed in a series.

Kung Fu: martial art style developed at the Shaolin Temple in China.

limbic system: brain system associated with emotions.

Magnetic Resonance Imaging: MRI. Provides images of the body's internal structures.

meditation: a relaxed yet energetically conscious state of mind.

mirror neurons: circuit of brain cells found on both sides of the brain.

mushin: Japanese for "no mind."

nondeclarative memory: procedural memory.

opiates: opium derivitives.

oxytocin: hormone secreted by the pituitary gland.

PET scans: 3-dimensional imaging technique.

pituitary gland: master endocrine gland located at the base of the brain, controlling the other endocrine glands.

plasticity: the ability of the brain to change itself.

pre-motor: part of the motor cortex located in the frontal lobe of the brain.

priming: occurs when exposure to certain stimulus, due to prior experience, produces certain responses.

procedural knowledge: knowledge consisting of the skills and operations we apply to declarative knowledge.

Prozac: an anti-depression drug.

receptors: cellular structure capable of binding other structures.

reflexive behaviors: behaviors activated by a reflex.

repressed memories: traumatic experiences unconsciously retained.

runner's high: euphoric feeling after running or some other aerobic activity.

schema: an outline, map, or model.

schematics: refers to a plan or map.

selective attention: the ability to choose what information you wish to attend to.

self: who you are and what you are feeling on the inside.

self-awareness: to be attentive to the self.

self-regulation: exercising control over various elements involved in achieving and/or maintaining personal goals.

sensei: martial arts teacher in Japanese. The word's root means to give birth.

serotonin: sometimes called the happy hormone because of its contribution to sleep and good moods.

Shaolin Temple: historically accredited as the birthplace of Zen in the martial arts.

Skinner box: well-known experiment of psychologist B.F. Skinner, to examine animal behavior.

Stroop Effect: demonstration of the way irrelevant information can interfere with the reaction time of a task.

suki: an interruptive thought.

sustained attention: ability to stay focused on any one thing.

testosterone: sex hormone mostly associated with men.

thalamus: area of the brain where sensory data (smells, tastes, the tactile feel of things as well as visuals and sounds) is first processed and then relayed to other parts of the brain.

top-down processing: information processing based on previous knowledge, expectations, and plans of action.

visualization: a process by which you use your mind's eye to see yourself or someone else within a specific experience, which may have already occurred or may occur in the future.

Xin-Yi: heart-mind.

BIBLIOGRAPHY

Amen, Daniel G. *Change Your Brain, Change Your Life.* New York: Three Rivers Press, 2004.

"Anne Treisman, PhD." Foundation for the Advancement of Behavioral and Brain Sciences. Retrieved February 5, 2009, from *www.fabbs.org/treisman_honor.html.*

"Attention/IQ/Academic Performance." The Transparent Corporation. Retrieved January 27, 2009, from *www.transparentcorp.coproducts.*

Barker, Lesley. "Who Invented the MRI?" eHow. Retrieved February 7, 2009, from *www.ehow.com/about_4599974_who-invented-mri.html.*

Begley, Sharon. *Train Your Brain, Change Your Mind.* New York: Ballantine, 2008.

Boyd, Kevin. "Testosterone Aids Older Men's Brains, Study Finds." University of California–San Francisco Medical Center. April 17, 2002. Retrieved July 27, 2008, from *http://pub.ucsf.edu/today/cache/news/200204161.html.*

"Brain Scans Show Meditation Changes Minds, Increases Attention." Board of Regents of the University of

Wisconsin System. June 25, 2007. Retrieved
November 2, 2008, from *www.news.wisc.edu/
13890*.

Carver, Joseph M., PhD. "Dopamine: Parkinson's Disease
and ADHD to Smoking and Paranoia." Retrieved
January 29, 2009, from *www.enotalone.com/article/
4115.html*.

"Classics in the History of Psychology: The Principles of
Psychology—William James (1890)." Retrieved
February 6, 2009, from *http://psychclassics.yorku.ca/
James/Principles/prin11.htm*.

"Cocktail Party Effect." Nation Master Encyclopedia.
Retrieved February 5, 2009, from
*www.nationmaster.com/encyclopedia/Cocktail-party-
effect*.

Cullen, Lisa Takeuchi. "How to Get Smarter, One Breath
at a Time." *Time*. January 10, 2006. Retrieved July
15, 2008, from *www.time.com/time/magazine/
article/0,9171,1147167,00.html*.

"Current Winner: 2009—Anne Treisman." University of
Louisville. Retrieved February 5, 2009, from *http://
grawemeyer.org/psychology/current-winner.html*.

Damasio, Antonio. *Descartes' Error: Emotion, Reason, and the
Human Brain*. New York: Penguin, 2005.

Diefendorff, James, Dr. "Perceived Self-Regulation and
Individual Differences in Selective Attention."
Journal of Experimental Psychology 4, No. 3 (1998):
228–247.

"Donald Eric Broadbent" *New World Encyclopedia*.
Retrieved February 5, 2009, from
*www.newworldencyclopedia.org/entry/
Donald_Broadbent*.

Dreifus, Claudia. "A Conversation With Joseph LeDoux: Taking a Clinical Look at Human Emotions." *New York Times Magazine*, October 8, 2002.

"Emotion Drives Attention: Detecting the Snake in the Grass." *Journal of Experimental Psychology* 130, No. 3 (2001): 466–478.

EPLab OnLine Measures. "Stroop Task." Retrieved February 5, 2009, from *www.snre.umich.edu/eplab/demos/st0/stroopdesc.html*.

Fernandez, Alvaro. "Training Attention and Emotional Self-Regulation: An Interview With Michael Posner." Retrieved November 29, 2008, from *www.sharpbrains.com/blog/2008/10/18/training-attention-and-emotional-self-regulation-interview-with-michael-posner*.

Gladwell, Malcolm. *Blink*. New York: Back Bay Books, 2005.

Goleman, Daniel. "The Brain Manages Happiness and Sadness in Different Centers." *New York Times Magazine*, March 28, 1995.

———. *Emotional Intelligence: Why It Can Matter More Than IQ*. New York: Bantam, 1995.

Green, Elmer E. and K.S. Oswakie. "Human Potential: The Significance of Brainwave Training." The International Society for Neurofeedback and Research. Retrieved February 2, 2009 from *www.isnr.org/uploads/Abstracts%20and%20Papers%20Pre1995.pdf*.

Hampson, Rick. "New York City Cheers Death-defying Rescuer." *USA Today*, January 4, 2007. Retrieved September 21, 2008, from *www.usatoday.com/news/nation/2007-01-02-subway-rescue_x.htm*.

"Hans Berger." StateUniversity.com (Net Industries).
Retrieved February 5, 2009, from *http://
encyclopedia.stateuniversity.com/pages/9409/Hans-
Berger.html.*

"History of MRI." The University of Manchester.
Retrieved February 7, 2009, from
*www.isbe.man.ac.uk/personal/dellard/dje/history_mri/
history%20of%20mri.htm.*

"How Do We Perceive Objects?" Princeton University
Department of Psychology. Retrieved February 5,
2009, from *https://weblamp.princeton.edu/~psych/
psychology/research/treisman/index.php.*

Hyams, Joe. *Zen in the Martial Arts.* New York: Bantam,
1982.

"IQ Test: Where Does It Come From?" Learninginfo.org
(Audiblox). Retrieved February 7, 2009 from *http:/
/iq-test.learninginfo.org/iq01.htm.*

Jackson, Maggie. *Distracted: The Erosion of Attention and the
Coming Dark Age.* Amherst: Prometheus, 2008.

Johnson, Steven. *Mind Wide Open.* New York: Scribner,
2004.

Kramer, Peter. *Listening to Prozac.* New York: Scribner,
2004.

Latham, Caroline. "Sharpbrains." October 10, 2006.
Retrieved October 18, 2008, from
*www.sharpbrains.com/blog/2006/10/10/brain-yoga-
stress-killing-you-softly.*

LeDoux, Joseph. *The Emotional Brain: The Mysterious
Underpinnings of Emotional Life.* New York: Simon
& Schuster, 1996.

Lupien, Sonia. "Stress, Memory, and Social Support."
McGill Reporter. Retrieved January 10, 2009, from
www.mcgill.ca/reporter/35/02/lupien/.

Lurie, A.R. *The Working Brain: An Introduction to Neuropsychology*. New York: Basic Books, 1976.

Marano, Hara Estroff. "Why We Dream." *Psychology Today*, March/April 2005.

"Meditate To Concentrate." *ScienceDaily*. Retrieved January 26, 2009, from *www.sciencedaily.com /releases/2007/06/070625193240.htm*.

"Meditation May Fine-Tune Control Over Attention." *ScienceDaily*. Retrieved January 26, 2009, from *www.sciencedaily.com /releases/2007/05/070507202029.htm*.

Neill, W.T. "Perception." *McGraw-Hill Yearbook of Science & Technology*. New York: McGraw-Hill, 1995.

Nicholson, Christy. "Memory and Consciousness: Consciousness to Unconsciousness and Back Again." *APS Observer* (Association for Psychological Science), August 2006. Retrieved June 9, 2008, from *www.psychologicalscience.org/observer/getArticle.cfm?id=2028*.

Othmer, Siegfried, PhD, and Caroline Grierson, RN. "Biofeedback: The Ultimate Self-Help Discipline." EEG Info. Retrieved January 10, 2009, from *www.eeginfo.com/research/articles/biofeedbackselfhelp.htm*.

Pfaff, Donald. *The Neuroscience of Fair Play: Why We (Usually) Follow the Golden Rule*. New York: Dana Press, 2007.

Posner, Michael and Mary. K. Rothbart. "Attention, Self-Regulation and Consciousness." Philosophical Transactions of the Royal Society of London B [Biological Sciences] 353, No. 1377 (29 November 1998): 1915–27.

Purvis, Karen L., and Rosemary Tannock. "Language Abilities in Children with Attention Deficit Hyperactivity Disorder, Reading Abilities and Normal Controls." Journal of Abnormal Child Psychology 25 (1997). Retrieved December 26, 2008, from *www.questia.com.*

"Runners' High Demonstrated: Brain Imaging Shows Release of Endorphins in Brain." *ScienceDaily.* Retrieved January 26, 2009, from *www.sciencedaily.com/releases/2008/03/080303101110.htm.*

Sakai, Jill. "Meditation May Fine-Tune Control Over Attention." Board of Regents of the University of Wisconsin System. May 8, 2007. Retrieved September 30, 2008, from *www.news.wisc.edu/13762.*

Schoenherr, Neil. "Flashbulb Memories." Washington University in St. Louis. November 5, 2003. Retrieved January 14, 2008, from *http://news-info.wustl.edu/tips/page/normal/516.html.*

Sohlberg, McKay Moore, and Catherine A. Mateer. *Introduction to Cognitive Rehabilitation: Theory and Practice.* New York: Guilford Press, 1989.

"Study Focuses on Progression of Menopause and Memory Loss." Yale New Haven Health System. November 17, 2003. Retrieved December 18, 2008, from *www.ynhh.org/healthlink/womens/womens_11_03.html.*

Tamm, Leanne, PhD, et al. "Can Attention Itself Be Trained? Attention Training for Children at Risk for ADHD." Retrieved December 10, 2008, from *www.sacklerinstitute.org/cornell/people/bruce.mccandliss/publications/publications/Tamm.etal.inpress.pdf.*

Vedhara, K., and J. Hyde, et al. "Acute Stress, Memory, Attention and Cortisol." *Psychoneuroendocrinology* 25, No. 6 (August 2000): 535–49.

Warm, Joel. "Are You Really Paying Attention? Doppler Sonography Helps Psychologists Measure Attention Levels." ScienceDaily. December 1, 2006. Retrieved November 10, 2008, from *www.sciencedaily.com/videos/2006/1212.*

"What is Neurofeedback?" EEG Info. Retrieved January 20, 2009, from *www.eeginfo.com/what-is-neurofeedback.htm.*

Whiting, Wythe L., and David J. Madden and Katherine J. Babcock. "Overriding Age Differences in Attentional Capture with Top-down Processing." *Psychology and Aging* 22, No.2 (June 2007): 223–232.

INDEX

ABOUT THE AUTHOR

Joseph Cardillo is a top-selling author in health, mind-body, and martial arts. His books *Be Like Water* and *Bow to Life* have inspired people of all ages and backgrounds worldwide. As an educator, he has taught more than 20,000 students at several colleges and universities, including the University at Albany and Hudson Valley Community College, where he is a professor of English and creative writing. He teaches classes in health and wellness at a wide range of other institutions, and has received two state university sabbaticals for work in consciousness studies. He regularly presents workshops and seminars based on his books. Joseph also writes a blog on attention training for *Psychology Today*. He and his family reside in New York state.

Visit *www.josephcardillo.com.*